# with fork & spoon

## By Annabel Langbein

Culinary Institute Press

For Ted, Sean and Rosie

CULINARY INSTITUTE
of NEW ZEALAND

Culinary Institute Press is the imprint of the Culinary Institute of New Zealand.


Published by:    Culinary Institute of

New Zealand

PO Box 99 068

Auckland

New Zealand, 1996.

Design: Wandering Stars

Photography: Shaun Cato-Symonds

Settings: Monique Lovering

Food: Annabel Langbein

Typeset and Production: Culinary Institute of New Zealand Ltd

Printed in Hong Kong.

ISBN: 0-473-03976-1

# Contents

**T**oday's food is fresh, informal, easily made, unpretentious and great tasting. To my mind it is a lot more "real" than any of the other culinary incarnations we have seen in the last 100 years. "Real" in the sense that it demands and presents really good quality fresh ingredients, not necessarily expensive ones, and it delivers good honest flavours. "Eat me" it begs, rewarding with satisfying good tastes that call you back for more.

These days it is far more fashionable to serve up something rustic and hearty like a mountain of flavoursome beans than a huge chunk of expensive rib eye beef. What a relief! This is the kind of food most people enjoy cooking and eating – it is fresh, unfussy, light in fat terms and remarkably easy to make as long as you start with good quality ingredients. With no last-minute fiddling, no complicated step by steps to execute some tricky triple-layered, triple-sauced plate, with disaster lurking in every step, the whole idea of cooking becomes so much more appealing.

The global pantry we have at our fingertips works wonders for making more interesting meals. Rice paper, couscous, polenta, balsamic vinegar, rice vinegar, fish sauce – you want it, the supermarket or the Asian foodstore or the local deli, has it. This tapestry of international flavourings and base ingredients makes cooking interesting fresh food so much easier and more accessible.

Very little in the way of expertise is required to create delicious food. You do need to taste your food as you make it, and understand before starting to prepare a new recipe what it is you are trying to achieve. You can follow the recipe exactly, or if you prefer, use the recipe merely as a guide if you wish to give a dish your own style.

I have given this book a seasonal focus to allow you to make the most of peak season produce, and to choose

foods which suit the weather of the day or season. After all, who wants to face a steaming, heavy bean and lamb shank cassoulet when outside the sky is as blue as a china cup and it is hot enough to fry an egg on the drive. We like cool, fresh food we can eat outdoors when it is hot, while for winter, out comes hearty rib sticking – keep the cold away – comfort fare.

There is something enormously appealing about choosing fresh foods which are in the peak of flavour, ripeness and supply, and creating simple but wonderful meals around them. Peak season harvests usually tend to be cheaper and fresher. Environmentally it is more sustainable to grow with nature's flow – less resources are required both in terms of production and transportation. And then there is the question, one which should be foremost, of taste – there is no way a tomato grown in the dark depths of winter will taste as good as one harvested in full summer ripeness.

At home we tend to eat very much by the seasons. I love picking something fresh from my vegetable garden and creating a meal around it. Today it was a cauliflower, which I cooked with a dash of water, then combined with hot pasta, tossing everything through with a big spoonful of winter parsley pesto and a little spoonful of harissa – both from out of the fridge. A grating of parmesan and a quick toss of some salad greens with really good oil and vinegar and we were eating. So simple and yet so very good.

We grew up as children around a philosophy that paid respect to nature's efforts. It is worth remembering that virtually everything we eat or would want to eat has started out at some stage as a seed, egg or spore, often taking months or even years to grow before we eat it. When nature has gone to such lengths to provide us with such extraordinary resources, it seems only right that we take a little care to prepare our food and make the time to enjoy it.

## HOW TO USE THIS BOOK

Most of the dishes in this book are designed to be served as stand alone meals. I tend to take a mix and match approach with my cooking – if extra people turn up I usually just prepare another dish or two and make everything go further or throw in another course. You'll find suggestions for extending a menu under the "make a menu match" heading which is at the end of most recipes. For times when you need special occasion ideas, look to the photo pages with menus; there are a few time-consuming recipes in this book – like the cassoulet and the bouillabaisse. These dishes are great for special occasions so we have given them special menus.

Before you start to cook, read the whole recipe through, get everything you will need out on the bench and prepare the ingredients in the order listed as stated next to the ingredient. So if it says 1 onion, diced, you dice up the onion and have it ready to use. That way you won't get to the end of the recipe and find you need to have cooked potatoes and there are none ready. Feel comfortable about what it is you are setting out to achieve and what you need to do to get there – I often read the recipe aloud to myself before I start so I feel clear about what I need to do and how (the neighbours thought I lost it years ago!)

As you browse through this book you will see it is divided into four seasonal chapters. Each season opens with a spread of ideas for different flavour boosters, toppings, spreads and platter ideas. These are multi-purpose tastes you can quickly and easily make to have on hand in the fridge so that you can whip together interesting snacks and starters, and add more zing to your everyday cooking. The salsa verde in the summer chapter for example, makes a great sandwich filling. You can toss it through pasta with some lightly-cooked seasonal vegetables, spread it on a piece of fish before cooking, or lace it through mayonnaise for a great tasting dip.

At the end of each seasonal chapter you will find a spread on breads to make and ideas for ready made breads like fresh tortillas – both of which you can use to extend a meal or as a starting point for a meal.

Within each chapter you'll find a page which gives you an update on our current favourite starches – couscous, polenta, mash and noodles.

Where practical, measures are given in cups or spoons. A metric 250ml cup is used, 1 tbsp=15ml, 1 tsp=5ml.

The recipes have been tested in a conventional oven. If you use fan-bake remember it is 10-15°C hotter and adjust temperatures and/or cook times accordingly.

The book is indexed in various categories – you can look for a recipe by its name, by its principal ingredient or by the style of recipe it is – a dressing/spread or a vegetable/vegetarian dish.

## THE GLOBAL PANTRY

Most of us keep a pantry of long-life dry goods, spices, seasonings, cans and basic staples like rice and pasta. Having a well-organised pantry is the key to making good food fast. It is worth going through your pantry like you do your wardrobe occasionally and ditching anything that you have never used and can't ever imagine using – the 10-year-old can of snails (I have one), and the chartreuse green jar of lime cucumber pickle (ditto). Before you chuck anything read this section to make sure what you are about to throw out is not in fact really useful.

In addition to all the stuff we know we should have, like oils – extra virgin and pure olive, soy or salad and sesame, vinegars – red and white wine and balsamic, canned tomatoes, tomato paste, canned beans, tuna, anchovies, olives, Dijon mustard, dried Chinese mushrooms, hoisin sauce, soya sauce and oyster sauce, coconut milk, various forms of chilli and chilli sauces and the gambit of dried spices and herbs (stored in sealed containers and replenished regularly), the following are some key long life items you will find extremely useful.

## Cardamom

Available in the pod, as seeds or ground. I prefer to use seeds and roughly grind them, or take the seeds from the pods. Great for flavouring cakes and biscuits as well as curries, tagines and marinades. Store in an airtight container.

## Fennel Seeds

Can be collected from wild plants and dried. Use in cakes and biscuits, curries, tagines and spice mixtures.

## Fish Sauce

The soya sauce of South East Asia, fish sauce is not unlike the garum used so widely by the Ancient Romans. Smells dreadful, keeps for ever and is fabulous – use 1-2 tbsp in a curry, salad, sauce or dressing for an amazing lift. It is very salty so taste food before adding extra salt – the *Thai Squid* brand is good and not too salty.

## Miso

This protein rich paste made from fermented soya beans and a grain - usually rice, is used daily in Japan. Mix with stock for a nourishing soup, add to marinades and sauces. Store in the refrigerator; keeps well for years.

## Nori

Seaweed wrapper made of laver seaweed, used to wrap sushi. Look for sushi grade. Also sold shredded for garnish in Asian food stores. Keeps for years unopened. Once opened it absorbs moisture and may soften.

## Rice Paper

Paper thin and super brittle, rice paper comes in various sizes of round, square and triangular pieces, with about 45-50 pieces per pack. This Southeast Asian pastry wrapper needs to be softened before use. Dip individual sheets quickly into hot water or brush both sides with hot water, and after a minute or two the sheets will be soft and workable. They can then be filled and served fresh or deep fried.

## Rice Wine Vinegar

Made from sake it has a mild sweet taste and is good in Asian dishes or as a replacement for lemon juice in dressings.

## Saffron

Wonderfully aromatic, saffron is the queen of spices, infusing foods with a rich heady flavour that cannot be copied. The dried stigma of a certain crocus flower (Crocus Sativus) native to the Eastern Mediterranean, it is the world's most expensive spice. Iranian brands are good and often cheaper. A deep rich red colour denotes good quality. Add to hot liquid to release colour and flavour, or dry until crisp and then crumble finely.

## Star Anise

Similar in flavour to anise seed but no relation, this pretty eight-pointed star seed capsule can be added to sweet syrups for fruits such as figs and pears, and used in marinades and Asian style sauces. The seeds are a component of 5 spice powder.

## Tamarind

The pulp of the seed pod of a tropical tree, tamarind has a unique sweet sour flavour – a bit like dates mixed with lime. It is commonly used in Asian, Indian and sometimes in Latin American cooking to give a sour flavour. If you buy it in a block with the seeds in it, cover with very hot water (about $1/4$ cup per walnut-sized ball), soak for 15 minutes then with your fingers work it with the soaking liquid into a purée, discarding the seeds. In the block or as a concentrate tamarind will keep indefinitely. Substitute 50/50 lime juice and molasses.

## Wasabi

The fiery Japanese horseradish used primarily as a condiment for sushi and sashimi. Sold as a paste or powder – thin with water to a paste as you would mustard. Mix a teaspoon with 2-3 tablespoons soy sauce for a dipping sauce.

*Vietnamese*

*Glass Noodle*

*Rolls, page 13*

# Summer

**A seat on the verandah,**

**a good book,**

**and a big wedge of juicy watermelon**

are the sum of simple pleasures. All we want is to be outdoors, no fuss, no bother, cool fresh eating. With its "just add water" approach couscous takes our fancy – we serve it perfumed with saffron, dates and almonds or piled high with quickly grilled summer vegetables, as a partner to outdoor barbecues.

We like gobal food we can make ahead and eat later – Sushi, Vietnamese Salad Rolls, Asian Deli Noodles, Mediterranean Lamb Sticks, and Spiked Chilli Mussels. Fridge stocks of pestos, salsas, and Slow-Roasted Tomatoes smarten up salads, dressings, marinades and slices of fresh crusty bread. Outdoors our barbecues go light with small portions of tasty meats, served atop spiked pineapple, peppers and mint or golden paw paw, lime and fresh coriander. We cook perfect beef by the fillet, and use it to make finger rolls stuffed with Salsa Verde, pack it into picnics along with scrummy meatloaves and layered chicken pies, and the freshest summer fruits. Summer's food says "eat me now" with vibrant abandon. It gives you every excuse to be outdoors, to go on a picnic and have a holiday.

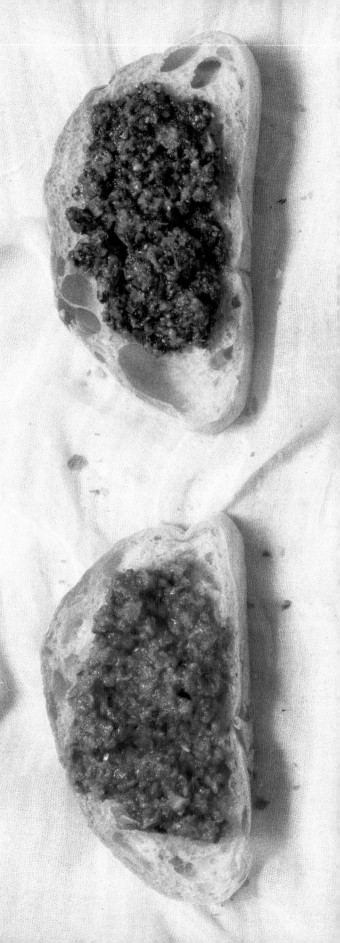

*S*ummer's rich full flavours
make for an easy life. What could be simpler than a
wedge of fresh crusty country loaf with a scrummy little
topping. Grill the bread first for Italian style bruschetta
or just serve fresh.

## Hot and Spicy Red Salsa

*A useful summer salsa to make when peppers are cheap and
plentiful. It can be mixed through dressings or combined with
mayonnaise or sour cream for a dip.*

**Purée** flesh of 3 roasted peppers, pith and seeds removed,
with 2 cloves garlic, 1-2 tbsp hot pepper or hot chilli sauce to
taste, salt to taste, 1 tsp fine black pepper, 1/4 cup olive oil and
1 large bunch coriander leaves and soft stems; blend until
smooth. **Stored** in the fridge with a layer of oil on top it will
keep for 2 weeks. **Makes about 1¹/₂ cups.**

## Slow Roasted Tomatoes

*Slow baking concentrates the flavour of tomatoes, giving
them an incredible richness and a lovely, almost creamy
texture. Use oval Italian tomatoes which are pulpier than
other varieties. Serve them up on bread, toss through roasted
vegetables or pasta, make a salad with slices of fresh
mozzarella and rocket or watercress leaves, or purée with
chicken stock and a little chilli for a hot or cold soup.*

**Preheat** oven to 170°C. **Place** 6 Italian tomatoes (oval),
halved lengthwise, cut side facing up into a baking dish so
they fit snugly. **Mix** together 2 tbsp extra virgin olive oil, 1
tbsp balsamic vinegar, 1 tsp sugar, ¹/₂ tsp salt and several
grinds of black pepper. **Pour** over tomatoes. **Bake** for 1¹/₂
hours. **Remove** and allow to cool. **Serve** on crusty bread.
Make up a big batch for anytime use through the summer.
They keep in the fridge for 2-3 weeks if covered with oil.

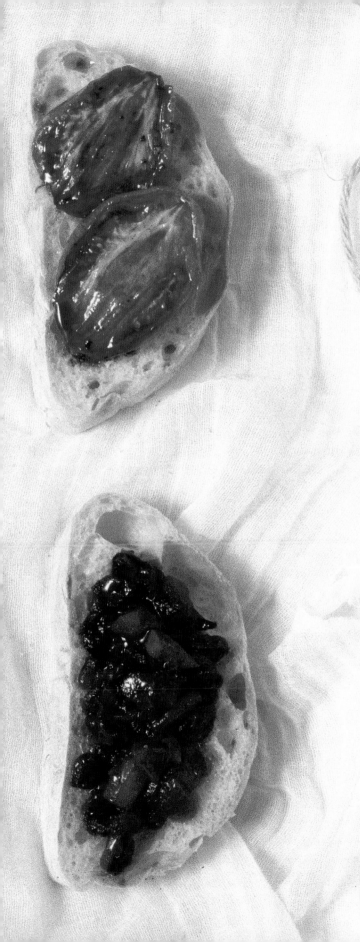

## Bengal Peach Chutney

*When peaches are in peak supply, make a brew of this spicy chutney. Use it to lift winter casseroles and tagines and serve in the summer as a spread or mixed through dressings.*

**Peel,** de-stone and cut up 3kg ripe peaches. **Combine** in a big heavy bottomed pot with 1kg brown sugar, 750g raisins or dates, 3 chopped onions, 3 tbsp crushed garlic, 3 tbsp grated fresh root ginger, 1 tbsp cinnamon, 3-4 whole cardamoms, 4 chillies or 1-2 tsp chilli powder, 2 tbsp salt and 6 cups malt vinegar. **Bring** to a boil then reduce heat to a low simmer and cook for about 1½-2 hours until the mixture is thick and pulpy, taking care mixture does not catch near end of cooking. **Bottle** in small sterilised jars and seal with a screwtop lid. **Keeps** for months. **Makes 5 small jars.**

## Salsa Verde

*This useful green sauce is a summer fridge staple. Mix with mayonnaise or vinaigrette for a great dressing for all manner of salads. Serve straight up on green beans, barbecued meats and bread. Or spread onto thin slices of rare beef and roll up.*

**Blend** together until smooth, 1 packed cup parsley leaves, ½ packed cup mint leaves, 1 bunch chopped chives, ¾ cup olive oil, ¼ cup capers, 3 cloves garlic, 2 tsp Dijon mustard, 2-3 tbsp lemon juice, ¼ medium onion, chopped, and one small can anchovies. **Store** in the fridge. **Keeps** for several weeks. **Makes about 1½ cups.**

## Summer Fruit Salsa

*Serve with barbecues and grills. Prepare just before using.*

**Combine** 2 cups diced fresh fruit e.g. peaches, strawberries, plums, pawpaw, kiwifruit or mangoes, with 2-3 tbsp fresh lime juice, ¼ cup chopped fresh mint or coriander, 1-2 minced chillies, salt, pepper and a tiny pinch of sugar. **Add** a little finely diced onion if desired. Use within 6-8 hours. **Makes 2 cups.**

## Shrimp, Tomato, Basil and Avocado Soup

*When we were children my mother used to make a shrimp and tomato cocktail which she served for special occasions. Here's my update on the idea, served as a chilled soup.*

**TO PREPARE:** 5 minutes

**1kg ripe tomatoes,** preferably Italian kind

**2 tsp sugar**

**2 large handfuls fresh basil,** removed from stems **or 1 tbsp basil pesto**

**salt & fine black pepper to taste**

**2 tsp balsamic vinegar or tarragon or spiced vinegar**

**2 tbsp extra virgin olive oil,** to taste

**good shake of hot sauce to taste**

**flesh of 1 firm but ripe avocado,** diced

**2 cups medium to large cooked shrimps,** thawed and halved

**1 cup tomato juice,** to thin, more or less to taste

**Pierce** tomato skins in several places with a fork, place in a bowl and cover with boiling water.

**Leave** for about 2 minutes, turning once or twice, then drain, peel and discard skins.

**Place** tomatoes in a blender or food processor with sugar, basil, salt and pepper, vinegar, olive oil and hot sauce.

**Purée** until smooth. Transfer to a bowl and mix in avocado and shrimps.

**Mix** in tomato juice, thinning to the consistency you prefer. I like mine quite thick.

**Chill** for at least 1 hour before serving.

**Serves 4.**

**Make a menu match with:** *Mediterranean Summer Couscous with Barbecue Lamb.*

## Spanish Tomato Salad

*In Spain when you sit down in a restaurant over the summer months you are often served a complimentary platter with slices of rustic bread, cloves of peeled garlic, some ripe sweet tomato halves, a little bottle of extra virgin olive oil, salt and a pepper grinder. You rub the garlic cloves over the bread, then rub the tomato into the bread, season with salt and pepper and drizzle lightly with the oil. It's a great way to wait for your meal. At home over the summer we often make a weekend lunch on the run out of it. The following recipe puts the idea into salad form for easy eating. It relies on really ripe, sweet, summer tomatoes so don't try making it when tomatoes are out of season. It will keep for up to 2 hours before being served but tastes at its very best within an hour.*

**TO PREPARE:** 5 minutes

**4 sweet ripe summer tomatoes,** cores removed and flesh diced finely

**1 small clove garlic,** peeled and finely crushed

**1 tsp brown sugar**

**2 tbsp extra virgin olive oil**

**several basil leaves,** torn in small pieces

**1-2 tsp balsamic vinegar,** to taste

**salt & freshly ground black pepper to taste**

**Combine** all ingredients in a bowl, season to taste with salt and pepper.

**Serve** on lightly grilled country bread or as a topping for fresh crusty bread or bruschetta.

**Serves 6-8.**

## Vietnamese Glass Noodle Rolls

*Pretty and light, these little rolls taste wonderfully clean and fresh. The shrimps can be replaced with cooked chicken, or left out entirely, and other salad ingredients added such as cucumber or sprouts.*

**TO PREPARE:** 15 minutes + soaking

**1 large handful clear glass noodles**

**2 spring onions,** finely sliced

**1 cup lettuce leaves,** freshly sliced

**¼ cup coriander or mint,** finely chopped

**1 large carrot,** peeled and shredded or grated

**1-1½ cups cooked shrimps,** roughly chopped

**1 tsp sugar**

**1 tbsp fish sauce**

**1 tsp sweet Thai chilli sauce**

**8 sheets of rice paper**

**Soak** noodles in warm water for 15 minutes. Drain thoroughly. Place in bowl. Mix in vegetables, herbs and shrimps.

**Mix** sugar, fish sauce and sweet Thai chilli sauce in a jar.

**Pour** over salad and mix through until everything is evenly combined.

**Dip** each rice paper sheet one at a time into hot water, just to wet. Lay on a damp clean tea towel (they will soften to a rollable texture in about 1 minute).

**Take** a small handful of filling and form a 3cm band across one edge of each prepared sheet of rice paper.

**Roll** up tightly to enclose the filling, folding in ends as you go, like an envelope. Refrigerate until ready to serve.

**Slice** each roll into 4-5. Arrange on a serving platter and accompany with dipping sauce.

**Makes 35-40 pieces.**

## Dipping Sauce

**Mix** 3 tbsp fish sauce, 1 tbsp sugar, 2 tbsp rice wine vinegar and 1 tbsp sweet Thai chilli sauce.

## Asian Deli Noodles

*The dressing for this great little salad is likely to become a kitchen staple – it's just so useful and delicious, and it keeps for weeks in the fridge. Drizzle it over barbecued or grilled meats, mix it through stir-fries, use as a marinade for pork ribs and chicken, or serve it here as I have done as a dressing for noodles, which make a great barbecue accompaniment.*

**TO PREPARE:** 5 minutes    **TO COOK:** 5-10 minutes for noodles

**Asian Deli Sauce:**
**2 tbsp soya or safflower oil; 3 cloves garlic,** peeled and chopped; **2cm piece root ginger,** minced or grated; **2 tbsp soya sauce; 1-2 tbsp sweet Thai chilli sauce,** to taste; **1 tbsp fish sauce; 2 tbsp peanut butter; 2 spring onions,** chopped; **handful of coriander leaves.**
**Salad:**
**500g Chinese noodles,** e.g. udon noodles, rice noodles **or spaghetti**
**½ cup peanuts,** roasted
**Salad Garnish** (use all or some of the following): **2 spring onions,** finely chopped; **¼ cup fresh coriander or mint,** chopped; **1 pkt mung bean sprouts; ½ cucumber,** cut in small batons; **1 red pepper,** diced.

**Purée** oil with all flavourings, peanut butter and herbs until semi-smooth for the Asian Deli Sauce.

**Prepare** noodles according to manufacturer's instructions. Drain and cool.

**Place** cooked noodles in a large bowl. Mix through dressing to combine. Mix through garnish ingredients.

**Serve** at room temperature. If planning to prepare ahead, add a little extra oil to dressing to stop noodles sticking.

**Serves 6.**

**Variation:** add cooked chicken or shrimps to salad for a meal in one.

**Make a menu match with:** *Barbecue Thai Chicken.*

# After Tennis and a Swim

*Pizza Bread Pinwheels*

*Smoked Chicken, Strawberries, Peaches and Summer Herbs*

*Greek Lemon Syrup Cake and fresh raspberries*

## Smoked Chicken, Strawberries Peaches and Summer Herbs

*This salad sings of summer. It's one of those great spur of the moment meals you can throw together if people arrive unexpectedly and you want to feed them something fresh and yummy. Any stone fruit, pawpaw or melon can be used. Using home-smoked chicken makes a real difference – see page 26 for the easy instructions on how to do this.*

**TO PREPARE:** 15 minutes    **TO COOK:** 1 minute

**2-3 handfuls snow peas or 2 stalks celery,** sliced thinly

**4 smoked chicken breasts,** sliced **or flesh of 1 smoked chicken,** skin removed, meat shredded

**1 punnet strawberries,** halved and hulled if large

**2-3 peaches,** halved, stones removed, sliced in wedges

**2-3 tbsp fresh mint or tarragon or basil,** chopped

**Orange Mustard Dressing:**

**2 tbsp white wine vinegar**

**1 tsp Dijon mustard**

**1 tbsp honey**

**¼ cup orange juice,** preferably fresh

**salt & freshly ground black pepper to taste**

**Pour** boiling water over snowpeas or celery and stand 1 minute.

**Drain** and cool under cold water.

**Drain** and put in a large mixing bowl.

**Add** all other salad ingredients.

**Mix** salad dressing ingredients together and gently toss through the salad.

**Divide** salad between plates and serve at once.

**Serves 4 as a main, 6 as a starter.**

**Make a menu match with:** *Fresh crusty bread, and a ripe brie.*

## Tuna Salad with Green and White Beans

*I often cook up a big pot of white beans over the summer and store them in the freezer so I can whip together salads like this at the drop of a hat. Vary the formula with potatoes instead of beans, heating them, like the beans, with the flavours before combining in the salad.*

**TO PREPARE:** 3 minutes    **TO COOK:** 2 minutes

**2 tbsp extra virgin olive oil**

**3 tbsp Salsa Verde** (see page 11) **or pesto**

**finely grated rind and juice of 1 lemon**

**2 tsp fresh thyme or rosemary,** chopped

**2 cups cooked white beans,** if using canned, rinse and drain

**salt & freshly ground black pepper to taste**

**1 bunch green beans,** stalks removed (about 250g)

**1 x 250g can tuna in brine,** drained and roughly flaked

**½ cup good tasting olives**

**1 punnet cherry tomatoes or 2 large tomatoes,** cores removed, flesh diced

**small bunch rocket or other salad leaves,** washed and dried

**Place** olive oil, Salsa Verde, lemon rind, juice and thyme or rosemary in a frypan or pot.

**Add** cooked white beans and heat 2-3 minutes to infuse flavour of dressing through them.

**Season** with salt and pepper and place in a large bowl.

**Bring** a small pot of lightly salted water to the boil. Add green beans and boil 2 minutes.

**Drain** and cool in cold water. Put in bowl with white beans. Add flaked tuna, olives, tomatoes and salad leaves and toss everything gently to combine. Serve at once.

**Serves 4.**

**Make a menu match with:** *Naan Bread.*

## Sushi Rice

*Sushi is such an easy thing to make, provided you have the right ingredients. This sushi rice can be prepared well ahead of time, as can the rolls themselves.*

**TO PREPARE:** 2 minutes + 30 minutes standing **TO COOK:** 30 minutes

**1 cup short grain rice,** e.g. Japanese sushi rice

**3 tbsp rice wine vinegar**

**1 tbsp sugar**

**2 tsp salt**

**Wash** rice then stand in cold water for 30 minutes. Drain thoroughly.

**Heat** together the vinegar, sugar and salt, in a small pot, stirring until dissolved. Put to one side.

**Place** rice in a medium size pot with a tight fitting lid and cover with 1 cup water.

**Boil** over high heat. As soon as rice comes to the boil, reduce the heat to lowest setting, cover pot and cook for 12 minutes.

**Remove** from heat and stand 15 minutes without uncovering. Mix through vinegar seasoning with a fork.

**Turn** out onto a large, flat, clean tray to cool. If you have time, use a fan to quicken cooling of the rice. The rice is now ready to use. It can be refrigerated for up to 48 hours, covered in plastic wrap to prevent drying. To stop it sticking to your hands when you are assembling sushi, wet your hands with cold water, then clap to remove any excess water before picking up rice.

**Makes** 2 cups cooked rice, enough for 6 filled sushi rolls or about 36 small sushi rice balls. Recipe doubles easily.

## Gingered Sushi Prawns

**Mix** cooked, seasoned sushi rice with $1/2$ cup finely diced cucumber and 3 tbsp finely chopped pickled ginger.

**Spoon** teaspoonfuls onto large prawn tails which have been pan-fried in a little sesame oil. **Makes enough for about 40.**

## Salmon and Avocado Sushi Rolls

*These are a favourite amongst sushi fans. You can also make them with smoked salmon if preferred.*

**TO PREPARE:** 10 minutes

**6 sheets nori seaweed,** sushi grade

**1 quantity cooked sushi rice**

**a little wasabi paste,** thinned with a little water

**150-200g freshest raw salmon,** skin and bones removed, cut in finger strips

**flesh of 1 large firm but ripe avocado,** mashed

**Toast** the shiny side of the nori by passing over an open flame – the nori will become crisp and develop flavour. Lay one sheet of nori on a bamboo mat or clean tea towel.

**Place** a handful of rice on a Nori sheet and pat out until rice covers all but a 5cm wide strip at the top edge of each nori sheet.

**Dip** your finger into thinned wasabi paste and about 4cm from the nearest edge of the rice, rub a line of wasabi from the left side to the right to give a thin flavour strip.

**Lay** salmon strips 2-3 thick along the wasabi line.

**Spread** a little mashed avocado on top of the salmon. Starting with the edge nearest you, roll up as tightly as possible using a sushi mat or teatowel to help roll tightly. When you get to the rice border, wet the remaining nori and then roll up.

**Chill** for at least 30 minutes, or up to 24 hours.

**Serve** each roll sliced crosswise into 6 pieces and accompany with a dipping sauce.

**Makes 36 pieces.**

**Make a menu match with:** *Warm sake.*

## Sushi Dipping Sauce

**Mix** $1/4$ cup soya sauce, preferably Japanese with 1 tbsp wasabi paste.

*Salmon and Avocado Sushi Rolls*

# Seared Sesame Salmon On Udon Noodles

*If you are out to impress, this is a great dish to serve. It looks and tastes sensational. The idea comes from talented young Auckland chef, Nick Huffman, and is based on a recipe he taught at one of our cooking classes. Slices of perfect salmon with a nifty sesame seed crust sit atop a bed of noodles with shredded seaweed, spring onions and a light Japanese dressing. Everything can be done ahead of time, ready for a quick last minute assembly. Take special care not to cook salmon for too long at the first stage – all you want to do is cook the egg white onto the salmon so the sesame seeds stick. If you overcook it you won't be able to cut the salmon so neatly. I buy fresh udon noodles at the local Asian food store and keep them in the fridge.*

**TO PREPARE:** 15 minutes and chilling  **TO COOK:** 4-5 minutes

**400-500g fillet of salmon,** skin and bones removed

**1 egg white**

**1 tbsp each white and black sesame seeds**

**2 tbsp oil**

**500g packet fresh udon noodles or cooked spaghetti**

**½ cup shredded nori,** buy shredded from Asian food stores

**2 spring onions,** finely sliced

**1 recipe Japanese dressing**

**Cut** salmon into 4 even-sized pieces.

**Brush** top of each piece with egg white.

**Combine** white and black sesame seeds in a shallow bowl and press side of salmon with egg white on, into seeds to fully cover the top.

**Heat** oil in a large frypan and brown salmon on seed side only, over high heat, about 30 seconds.

**Remove** and place seed side up in a single layer on a tray. Refrigerate immediately.

**Preheat** oven to 200°C. Prepare noodles. If using fresh udon noodles, bring to room temperature and then carefully separate with your fingers. Mix through a teaspoon of oil to prevent sticking.

**Microwave** or steam noodles to heat through.

**Slice** each piece of cold salmon into 3-4 equal slices.

**Lay** slices slightly overlapping in groups of 3-4 on a baking tray, greased or lined with baking paper. Bake for 3-4 minutes or until salmon is just warmed through.

**Mix** noodles with shredded seaweed, spring onions and ¾ of the Japanese dressing. Divide amongst 4 shallow bowls.

**Lift** salmon slices carefully off oven tray and arrange on top of noodles. Spoon over rest of dressing. Serve at once. This dish can also be served at room temperature.

**Serves 4 as a main and 6-8 as a first course.**

## Japanese dressing

**Mix** together in a small jar 3 tbsp rice wine or white wine vinegar, 3 tbsp salad or canola oil, 2 tbsp water, 2 tbsp oil, 1 tbsp soya sauce e.g. Kikkoman, 1 tsp sesame oil.

**Dressing** will keep for weeks in the fridge; recipe easily doubles or trebles. Use it to dress any kind of Asian salad.

**Make a menu match with:** *Cheat's Consommé with Chilli, Coriander and Wontons; and Harvest Fruit Brûlée.*

---

### PRE-COOKING PASTA AND NOODLES

Don't be put off from serving pasta or noodles when entertaining, thinking you will need to be cooking at the last minute. They can successfully be cooked ahead of time, following manufacturer's instructions. Once cooked, place under cool water, then drain and mix through a little oil to prevent sticking. To reheat, simply cover tightly and microwave 2-4 minutes, or pour over boiling water and leave for 30 seconds before draining.

# Who's Coming to Dinner?

Cheat's Lavosh with Boursin Cheese

Seared Salmon on Udon Noodles

Lightly boiled beans or asparagus

Prune and Orange Soufflés

*Flash Roasted Fish*

*with Olive Paste and Red Pepper Sauce*

## Spiked Chilli Mussels with Lemongrass

*Fresh mussels have to be one of the cheapest sources of protein around, and they taste so good. At their easiest, put them into a pot with a little extra virgin olive oil and a handful of fresh herbs, cover tightly and cook until they open, then squeeze over a little lemon juice. This variation on the theme cooks them in a flavoursome Asian broth.*

**TO PREPARE:** 8 minutes    **TO COOK:** 8-10 minutes

**24-30 fresh live mussels,** scrubbed and beards removed

**1 cup Riesling or other fruity white wine**

**1 cup stock, or water**

**1 spring onion,** minced

**1 tsp root ginger,** finely chopped

**1-2 tsp hot chilli sauce**

**1 tbsp lemongrass,** minced **or 1 tsp finely grated lemon rind,** no pith

**2 tbsp fresh coriander,** chopped

**2 tbsp lemon juice**

**Place** mussels in a big pot with white wine and stock (use a good stock cube if fresh is unavailable, as mussels have lots of flavour of their own). Cover tightly and cook until they open.

**Remove** mussels from liquid and put to one side. Add spring onion, ginger, hot chilli sauce and lemongrass or rind to mussel liquid and simmer for 2-3 minutes.

**Add** mussels back to pot for 1-2 minutes to heat through.

**Mix** in coriander and lemon juice. Adjust seasonings to taste. Serve at once.

**Serve** 6-8 mussels per serve with a little broth. Mussels can also be chilled for 2-3 days and served cold.

**Serves 4-5.**

**Make a menu match with:** *Pizza topped with herbs, garlic and olive oil.*

## Flash Roasted Fish with Olive Paste and Red Pepper Sauce

*This is a fabulous dish to make when you get some lovely fresh fish and want a quick elegant summer dinner. The sauce will keep for 3 or 4 days in the fridge and is also nice mixed through pasta with seafood, spooned onto grilled scallops or served with steaks.*

**TO PREPARE:** 10 minutes    **TO COOK:** 5-8 minutes

**Red Pepper Sauce:**

**flesh of 2 roasted red peppers**

**¼ cup stock or orange juice**

**salt & freshly ground black pepper to taste**

**4 x 180-200g fresh boneless fish pieces,** e.g. salmon, bluenose, hapuka

**¼ cup good quality olive paste, black or green**

**large bunch green beans,** stem ends removed

**Preheat** oven to 250°C.

**Purée** red peppers with stock or juice until smooth. Season to taste with salt and pepper. Reserve to one side.

**Place** fillets in a lightly oiled baking dish and fold under shallow ends. Spread with olive paste.

**Heat** about ½ cup water in a pot and when it boils add beans – they will take about the same time as the fish to cook.

**Bake** fish for 5-8 minutes until fish shows very little resistance when pressed. Check after 5 minutes. Do not overcook – the fish should still be slightly translucent in the centre, and not "give" too easily. While fish cooks, heat red pepper sauce.

**To serve,** spoon red pepper sauce into the centre of each plate. Top with fish and garnish with beans around the outside of the plate.

**Serves 4.**

**Make a menu match with:** *Shoestring oven fries, with fresh summer berries and Greek Yoghurt to finish.*

## Mediterranean Summer Couscous with Barbecue Lamb

*Tender lamb fillets marinate while you assemble the other ingredients for this meal in a salad. You could also make it with a butterflied leg of lamb, or barbecue chicken or beef. The recipe is easily doubled and is great for feeding a crowd with a stand alone dish.*

**TO PREPARE:** 20 minutes   **TO COOK:** 5 minutes

**4-6 lamb fillets**
**Marinade: 1 tsp ground cumin; finely grated rind of 1 lemon,** no pith; **2 tbsp lemon juice; 2 cloves garlic,** crushed; **1 tbsp oil.**
**Salad: 3 cups water; 1 tsp each turmeric, salt and harissa; 2 tbsp pesto**
**2 cups instant couscous**
**salt & freshly ground black pepper to taste**
**Salad garnish: 1-1½ cups fresh grapes or fresh apricots,** chopped; **2 spring onions,** finely sliced; **1 cup almonds,** toasted; **1 cup dates or figs,** finely chopped, **or other dried fruits; finely grated rind and juice of 1 orange,** no pith; **2-3 tbsp fresh basil or mint,** chopped.

**Mix** lamb fillets with marinade ingredients. Stand while preparing couscous.

**Place** water in pot with turmeric, salt, harissa and pesto. Bring to a boil. Remove from heat, add couscous and stir. Stand for 8-10 minutes until liquid is absorbed.

**Heat** a heavy pan or barbecue plate; season lamb with salt and pepper. Cook lamb 2-3 minutes until medium rare. Remove from pan and stand before slicing.

**Combine** grapes or apricots, spring onions, almonds, dates or figs, orange rind and juice in a large bowl. Mix through soaked couscous. Pile onto a serving platter.

**Angle** slice lamb fillets in 2cm pieces and pile on top of salad. Sprinkle over basil or mint.

**Serves 4-6.**

## Barbecue Thai Chicken with Fresh Paw Paw

*This is a great little marinade for any kind of poultry or meat. Remember to boil it before you pour over cooked chicken at the end. Marinades used for raw meats should not be combined with cooked meats for safety reasons. Double the recipe for a crowd.*

**TO PREPARE:** 5 minutes   **TO COOK:** 5 minutes + marinating time

**Marinade: ¼ cup lemon grass,** minced **or 1 tbsp finely grated lemon or lime rind; 2 tbsp brown sugar; 4 cloves garlic,** crushed; **3 tbsp fish sauce; 2 tbsp fresh lime or lemon juice; 2 tsp tamarind concentrate; 1-2 tsp chilli paste or minced chillies**
**6 boneless chicken breasts or 10-12 boneless thighs,** beaten out flat between 2 sheets of plastic wrap to 1.5 cm thickness
**1 large just-ripe pawpaw,** peeled, seeds removed, flesh sliced in wedges or **6-8 peaches,** sliced in wedges
**2 tbsp lemon or lime juice**
**¼ cup fresh coriander or mint,** chopped
**Optional: ½ cup cashews or peanuts,** toasted and chopped

**Combine** all marinade ingredients in a non-reactive bowl or clean plastic bag. Flatten chicken, add to marinade and mix to coat.

**Marinate** for 15 minutes or up to 2 hours in the fridge.

**Lift** chicken out of marinade, brushing excess marinade from chicken back into marinade. Reserve marinade.

**Preheat** a barbecue plate, grill or pan with a little oil.

**Cook** chicken about 1½ minutes each side. While chicken cooks heat marinade, boiling for 2 minutes.

**Mix** sliced pawpaw or peaches with lime or lemon juice and herbs and pile onto a serving platter. Top with chicken and spoon over hot marinade. Sprinkle with optional nuts.

**Serves 6.**

# Perfect Beef Fillet with Black Bean Salad

*Here's a crowd pleaser, great for a summer buffet, barbecue or picnic. The method for cooking the beef might sound odd but it is fantastic. There's no soaking for the beans, and both beans and beef can be cooked a day ahead if desired.*

**TO PREPARE:** 10 minutes    **TO COOK:** 2 hours (beans) 24-30 minutes (beef)

**3 cups black beans,** washed

**Dressing: ³/₄ cup spiced vinegar; 2 tbsp sugar;**

**1 tbsp ground cumin; 3 tbsp sweet Thai chilli sauce;**

**4 cloves garlic,** crushed; **1¹/₂ tsp salt; 1 tsp fine ground**

**black pepper; ¹/₄ cup oil; ¹/₄ cup water.**

**Salad:**

**1 large red onion,** finely chopped

**1 large avocado,** diced

**3 tomatoes,** cores removed and flesh diced

**2 cups corn kernels**

**1 large red pepper,** finely chopped

**2 spring onions,** finely sliced

**¹/₂ cup mint, coriander or parsley,** chopped

**Beef:**

**1 fillet beef about 1-1.2kg**

**2 tbsp each brown sugar and mustard**

**salt & freshly ground black pepper to taste**

**Place** black beans in a large pot and cover with cold water. Bring to a boil, reduce heat and simmer 2 hours or until tender.

**Boil** together all dressing ingredients for 2 minutes.

**Drain** cooked beans, mix through hot dressing and leave to cool. Beans can be prepared to this point up to 48 hours ahead of time and kept in the fridge. When ready to serve mix through prepared salad ingredients. Serve at room temperature.

**Preheat** oven to 250°C. Place beef fillet in a deep roasting dish, tucking under any narrow ends.

**Mix** sugar and mustard and spread over the top. Sprinkle with salt and pepper.

**Pour** hot water around beef to come half way up the sides of the fillet. Make sure there is enough water.

**Place** beef in hot oven for 12-15 minutes then turn off oven and leave for 12-15 minutes. Take out and feel. If it still feels very squidgy put back into oven for another 10-15 minutes (time will vary depending on size and thickness of fillet). Remove from oven and leave to cool in liquid. Slice when fully cool.

**Place** overlapping slices of meat around edge of a large serving plate with a pile of beans in the middle.

**Serves 8.**

**Make a menu match with:** *Pizza Bread or Naan Bread.*

---

### HOW TO TELL WHEN MEAT IS COOKED

*Dense pieces of meat such as beef fillet or lamb racks have a varying texture depending on the state to which they are cooked. Use the texture of the flesh at the base of your thumb – the Mount of Venus, as a comparison for rare to well cooked meat and squeeze from the sides in the thickest part of the meat as your gauge.*

**"The Point"**– Relax your hand and feel the flesh at the base of your thumb – it will feel very squidgy – this is how raw meat feels. From here on for easy reference this area will be referred to as "the point".

**Rare meat** – Touch your thumb to your first finger – press "the point" – this is what meat feels like when rare.

**Medium rare** – touch your second finger and thumb together, and press "the point" – this is what medium rare meat feels like.

**Medium** – Touch your thumb to your third finger and press "the point" – this is what medium meat feels like.

**Well Done** – Touch your thumb to your little finger and press "the point" – this is what well done meat feels like.

## Chinese Glazed Ribs with Fresh Pineapple Salad

*Finger licking stuff. Another great marinade especially for pork. Use it also with satays, fillets or a whole loin.*

**TO PREPARE:** 7-8 minutes   **TO COOK:** 1 hour

**Marinade: 2 tbsp each garlic,** crushed; **root ginger,** grated; **2 tbsp hoisin sauce; 2 tbsp sherry; 1 tsp honey**

**1kg meaty pork ribs,** cut into 2-3 rib sections

**2 tbsp extra honey** for glazing ribs

**Salad: ½ red onion,** thinly sliced; **½ fresh pineapple,** peeled, core removed, thinly sliced; **½ cup fresh mint,** chopped; **1 red pepper,** finely diced.

**½ cup fresh orange juice**

**2 tsp sesame oil**

**Combine** marinade ingredients.

**Mix** through ribs in a non-reactive container and leave for at least 1 hour or up to 24 hours in the fridge, turning occasionally.

**Preheat** oven to 200°C.

**Place** ribs and marinade in a roasting dish, so they fit snugly.

**Cover** and bake for 40 minutes. Uncover, bake a further 15-20 minutes until shiny, brushing with honey and marinade a couple of times once uncovered to help glazing.

**While** meat cooks combine all salad ingredients in a bowl with orange juice and sesame oil. Pile onto a serving platter. Top with hot ribs.

**Serves 4-6.**

**Make a menu match with:** *Baked or roasted kumara.*

## Mediterranean Lamb Sticks

*A quick dip into boiling water sets these sticks for easy barbecuing. You can make them up a day ahead of time and have in the fridge ready for the hot plate. Vary the flavourings for other types of mince – the meatloaf mixture on the next page minus soaked bread is also delicious cooked this way. If meat has been frozen you will need an extra egg white.*

**TO PREPARE:** 10 minutes   **TO COOK:** 7-8 minutes

**500g fresh lean lamb mince**

**2 cloves garlic,** crushed

**½ cup olives,** chopped

**1 tsp salt**

**1 tbsp pesto**

**finely grated rind of ½ lemon,** no pith

**freshly ground black pepper to taste**

**1 egg white**

**a little oil to brush**

**Mix** all ingredients together by hand until well combined.

**With** wet hands mould about 1 tbsp of mixture onto disposable wooden chop sticks or barbecue skewers to evenly cover 4-5 cm length on the top of each stick.

**Boil** a large saucepan of water. Drop prepared skewers into boiling water for 1 minute, cooking 2-3 at a time. Repeat to par-cook all skewers.

**Leave** to cool. Sticks can be prepared to this point and refrigerated for up to 48 hours.

**Brush** with oil. Grill or barbecue until brown, about 5-6 minutes.

**Accompany** with Salsa Verde or Hot and Spicy Red Salsa.

**Makes 16.**

**Make a menu match with:** *Grilled or Roasted Vegetables, or Roasted Vegetable Couscous.*

## Home-Smoked Chicken

*The flavour of home-smoked chicken is exceptional and it is very easy to prepare. Sports shops usually sell untreated sawdust. You'll need an old deep roasting dish and a rack that fits inside. Smoked chicken will keep 4-5 days in the fridge.*

**Mix** together 2 tsp each brown sugar and salt. Rub 4 chicken breasts all over with this mixture.

**Sprinkle** a small handful of untreated sawdust evenly over the bottom of roasting dish. Arrange baking rack on top, place chicken on rack, leaving a little space between each piece. Cover dish very tightly with tin foil.

**Preheat** oven to 200°C. Once oven is hot, turn an electric element on high, or light gas burner onto high heat.

**Place** covered chicken dish on hot element (a little smoke may sneak out the sides, don't open to see). Smoke for 5 minutes.

**Transfer** to hot oven and cook for 10 minutes. Stand 3-4 minutes then uncover and remove – chicken should be perfectly cooked. If it is not fully cooked through simply return to hot oven for a few minutes more. Serve cool.

**Serves 4.**

**Make a menu match with:** *Salad greens, grapefruit segments, and lemon or lime-infused olive oil.*

## Home-Smoked Fish

*This can be prepared in the same way as home-smoked chicken but the cook time is less. Fish such as salmon and trout taste delicious when rubbed with a little whisky or vodka before cooking. Cooking varies according to size and thickness of fish. Leave the skin on to keep fish moist.*

**Rub** cut side of 1 side of salmon, trout or snapper with 2 tbsp salt. Leave for 30 minutes. This firms up flesh.

**Wipe** off salt, rub 2 tbsp whisky or vodka into flesh.

**Sprinkle** with 2 tsp brown sugar. Proceed as for chicken allowing 5 minutes on top of the stove and 3-5 minutes in a 200°C oven.

## Spicy Pork Meatloaf

*This recipe brings new meaning to the word meatloaf. Slice it up with summer greens for an easy lunch or holiday meal, or take it on summer picnics – it travels and slices well.*

**TO PREPARE:** 5 minutes    **TO COOK:** 50-60 minutes

**1 cup fresh breadcrumbs mixed with ½ cup milk**

**2 spring onions**

**4 cloves garlic,** chopped

**4 tbsp ginger,** chopped

**2 tsp finely grated lime or lemon rind**

**¼ cup fresh coriander,** chopped

**2 tbsp fish sauce**

**1 tsp salt**

**1 egg white**

**1kg lean pork mince, or beef mince**

**2 tbsp sweet Thai chilli sauce**

**Mix** bread and milk and leave to soak. Purée together spring onions, garlic, ginger, lime rind, fresh coriander, fish sauce, and egg white. Add soaked bread.

**Mix** by hand into pork or beef mince. Spoon mixture into a 20cm x 12cm loaf and press firmly.

**Unmould** onto a shallow baking tray. Brush top with chilli sauce and bake at 180°C for 50-60 minutes or until juices run clear when pricked and loaf feels bouncy when pressed with no give.

**Cool,** then refrigerate for at least 2 hours. When fully cold slice thinly.

**Serve** thin slices accompanied with extra sweet Thai chilli sauce. Meatloaf will keep in the fridge for 3-4 days. Raw mixture can be used to make meatballs or barbecue patties.

**Serves 6-8.**

**Variation:** use raw mixture for meatballs or barbecue patties.

**Make a menu match with:** *Asian Deli Noodles.*

COUSCOUS, *the North African staple, is one of the simplest foods to prepare and work with – all you need to do is add water. A type of semolina made from wheat grain, couscous evolved from the idea of steaming grain (originally barley) in the steam from the stew, so that only one cooking fire was needed.*

*Until quite recently couscous was prepared traditionally throughout the countries of the Mahgreb – Morocco, Tunisia and Algeria. Each family sent its wheat to the local mill to be ground to the desired fineness. They then rolled each dampened grain in flour to create tiny pellets. The grains are again moistened, lightly oiled and left to dry. The end result is tiny pale gold pellets which retain their individuality and are light and fluffy when cooked. These days the couscous we buy has been machine-rolled, and pre-cooked, requiring only a brief soaking in hot water or stock to fluff up. If you are going to steam it over a stew, soak it first in cold water for 5 minutes then transfer to a cheesecloth-lined steamer, steam for 15-20 minutes then fluff with a fork and season with salt and pepper. Otherwise simply pour over boiling water or flavoured stock, (I generally use $1^1/_2$ cups water for every cup couscous), season well with salt and pepper and add a dash of oil. Leave until liquid is fully absorbed (5-10 minutes), then fluff with a fork. Reheat in the microwave or in a steamer, or if you are using it for salads, serve at room temperature.*

*Couscous is traditionally served with spicy meat and vegetable stews. It also makes a great salad base and works well with a range of flavourings. Bulgur wheat can be substituted, but not cracked wheat – it is coarser and requires much longer cooking.*

## Saffron Date and Almond Couscous

*This pretty, light salad holds and transports well and is ideal for picnics as well as an accompaniment for barbecued or grilled meats.*

**In** a pot or heatproof bowl place a big pinch saffron threads, 1 tsp salt, lots of freshly ground pepper, and the finely grated rind of 1 lemon. **Pour** over 3 cups boiling water and mix in 2 cups instant couscous. **Stand** for about 10 minutes until liquid is fully absorbed. **Mix** in $1/_2$ cup toasted almonds, $1/_2$ cup chopped dates or raisins, $1/_4$ cup chopped mint, $1/_2$ cup orange juice and the juice of 1 lemon. **Reheat** in microwave for 3-4 minutes in a covered container if you wish to serve hot, or serve at room temperature.

**Serves 4-6.**

## Roasted Vegetable Couscous

*In this easy meal-in-one, the vegetables fast-roast with a little flavoured oil, while the couscous soaks. Vary the vegetables according to what is in your fridge or garden.*

**Preheat** oven to 220°C. In a roasting dish place 2 red onions cut in thin wedges, 1 bunch fresh asparagus spears, each spear cut in half, (tough ends snapped off and discarded), 5-6 canned artichokes, drained and chopped, 2 zucchini cut thinly on an angle and $1/_2$ cup black olives. **Mix** 2 tbsp olive oil with juice of $1/_2$ lemon, 2 cloves crushed garlic, 1 tbsp fresh chopped rosemary, 1 tsp chilli powder and 1 tbsp ground cumin. Pour over vegetables and mix through evenly. **Season** with salt and freshly ground pepper. **Place** in the hot oven and cook for 15-20 minutes until tender and lightly browned. While vegetables cook, place 1 cup instant couscous in a bowl with 1 tsp salt, lots of freshly ground pepper and finely grated rind of 1 lemon. **Pour** over $1^1/_2$ cups boiling water. Stand 10 minutes. Mix through roasted vegetables.

**Serves 2-4.**

# Chicken, Ham and Apricot Raised Picnic Pie

*Colleague and friend Jane Redfern is our resident pie expert. Her wonderful pie makes great summer picnic fare.*

**TO PREPARE:** 30 minutes   **TO COOK:** 1 hour

**Pastry: 3³/₄ cups high grade or all purpose flour;
³/₄ tsp salt; 1 tbsp icing sugar** (yes, it helps the lard);
**220g lard; 1 cup water.**

**6-8 thin slices ham**

**1 cooked size 8 chicken,** skin, bones and fat removed,
meat chopped, **or 500-600g cooked chicken meat**

**1 tbsp fresh tarragon,** chopped

**120g dried apricots,** soaked for 1 hour then drained

**1 cup chicken stock** mixed with **3 tsp gelatine**

**1 egg,** lightly beaten to glaze

**Sift** dry ingredients for pastry together in a bowl. Place lard and water in a large pot and bring to a boil.

**Remove** from heat and add to dry ingredients all at once and mix well. Put dough into plastic bag to cool for 5 minutes.

**Roll** out ²/₃ of pastry until smooth, on a lightly floured board. Cover the bottom and sides of a 22cm springform cake tin, so pastry overhangs top edge of tin and there are no gaps. Roll out remaining pastry to easily fit top of pie.

**Fill** pie with layers of ham, chicken mixed with tarragon, and apricots finishing with a layer of ham. Cover with pastry lid, sealing pastry very tightly, and crimping edges together so that no juices can escape.

**Preheat** oven to 200°C. Make a 1cm hole in middle of pie top and decorate pastry with pastry leaves. Brush with beaten egg and cook for 1 hour at 200°C or until pie is nicely golden. Leave to cool.

**Mix** gelatine with chicken stock, heating to dissolve. Pour into pie when pie is cold. Take out of tin when juices are set. Keep in the fridge; pie will keep 4-5 days.

**Serves 8-10.**

## Pizza Pinwheels

*This light chewy pizza dough makes a great base for little pinwheel rolls, filled with a savoury paste such as olive paste, sun dried tomato paste or pesto. I like to cook them in a non-stick cake tin as it gives the rolls a golden crunchy base.*

**TO PREPARE:** 15 minutes plus rising     **TO COOK:** 15-20 minutes

**1³/₄ tsp dried yeast**

**pinch of sugar**

**1¹/₃ cups warm** (not hot) **water**

**¹/₃ cup olive oil**

**3³/₄ cups high grade flour**

**1¹/₂ tsp salt**

**¹/₄ cup sundried tomato paste or olive paste**

**Stir** dried yeast and sugar into water in large mixing bowl.
**Stand** 5 minutes until foamy. Stir in oil.
**Mix** flour and salt in a big bowl. Add yeast mixture, beating well to get all the lumps out.
**Turn** out onto a lightly floured surface and knead until soft and satiny but not sticky – about 8 minutes.
**Roll** ball of dough around in a well oiled bowl to coat it with oil. Tightly seal bowl with plastic wrap and set aside in a warm, draught-free place. Let dough rise until nearly double in size, 30-45 minutes. Divide dough in half.
**Roll** each half out to a rectangle 32cm x 20cm. Spread each rectangle with sundried tomato paste or olive paste.
**Roll** up each rectangle along longest edge to form 2 neat long rolls.
**Cut** each roll in 2cm pieces. Place these pinwheels cut side down in a shallow well-oiled baking tray or 2 greased 25 cm, non stick baking tins, with about 1cm between each.
**Brush** with olive oil. Leave to rise in a warm place for about 30-40 minutes.
**Bake** at 200°C for 15-20 minutes until golden.

**Makes 2 dozen.**

*Chicken, Ham and Apricot Raised Picnic Pie and Pizza Pinwheels*

*Spice Seared Lamb with*

*Chickpea Purée and Eggplant, page 48*

# Autumn

**Saturated by a summer's sun, autumn flavours burst through – sweet, dense and ripe as they will ever be.**

As the air turns to crisp, we pack thermoses with hearty soups and head out to harvest the season's bounty, or picnic in autumn leaves. We roast to intensify the rich flavours of red peppers, tomatoes, eggplant, garlic and pumpkin. They fill our plates for easy grazing meals on Indian summer evenings and stock the fridge with tastes that will remind us of summer after it has long gone. Our efforts in simply turning on the oven emerge as warm salads with pears, onions and chicken, tender lamb racks with savoury crisp crusts, Spice Seared Lamb, golden eggplant slices and laden platters of roasted vegetables to serve with rich golden aïoli. The season's first walnuts find a home in fresh oil-free dressings flavoured with orange juice, and as crunchy salad garnishes toasted with a spicy crust. Polenta takes centre stage as our favoured starch – we eat it hot and wet with spicy stews and tagines and as grits flavoured with chilli and fresh coriander. Or leave it to cool and cut it up for the grill or the frypan, ready for a quick little sauce of freshly picked field mushrooms. As the nights cool down, we light the first fires and invite friends over for easy informal meals. Fruitful and mellow, there is a bite in the air that lets us know winter is around the corner. It's a time to stock up, put up and celebrate the harvest.

*P*ile it onto a platter – it's such an easy way to eat. Spread it out with fresh crusty breads and a good cheese or use as toppings for bread, crackers and crostini – great for pre-dinner nibbling.

## Boursin Cheese

*Use this versatile spread as a great filling for chicken breasts, melt over steaks for a quick sauce, or pop it onto a platter.*

**Purée** together 250g cream cheese, 2 cloves chopped garlic, 4 fillets of anchovies, 1 tbsp capers and $\frac{1}{4}$ cup cream. **Thin** with extra cream for a dipping sauce. Mixture will keep for a week in the fridge. **Makes 1¼ cups.**

## Greek Roasted Minted Carrots

*Serve these tasty carrots as part of any antipasto platter or hot as a vegetable accompaniment.*

**Preheat** oven to 220°C. **Peel** 6 large juicy carrots and cut into thin slices (about 1cm). **Place** in a large roasting dish. **Mix** in 2 tsp brown sugar, 2 tbsp olive oil, 2 cloves crushed garlic, 1 cup white wine, $\frac{1}{2}$ cup black olives, 2 tbsp balsamic vinegar and $\frac{1}{2}$ cup chopped fresh mint. **Spread** out evenly in dish. **Cook** for 35-45 minutes stirring occasionally until carrots are tender and lightly browned. Keeps 3-4 days in the fridge. **Serves 6.**

## Smoked Mackerel Pâté

*An easy pâté that makes great use of any hot-smoked fish. Serve it with crackers or as part of a platter.*

**Flake** 200g smoked mackerel or other hot-smoked fish e.g. snapper or salmon. **Place** half fish in a blender with 150g light cream cheese, $\frac{1}{4}$ cup lemon juice, freshly ground black pepper to taste and a good pinch cayenne pepper. **Purée** until smooth. **Mix** in remaining flaked fish. Pâté will keep 5-7 days in the fridge. **Makes 2 cups.**

## Eggplant Confit

*When eggplant is plentiful make up potfuls of this yummy eggplant brew. It will keep in the fridge for weeks. Purée for a great tasting dip, or serve chunky in sandwiches, as a salad accompaniment or as part of a platter.*

**Preheat** oven to 220°C. **Slice** 1 large eggplant in 1.5cm slices. **Drop** into a large pot of boiling water for 2 minutes, or microwave in a covered dish with 2 tbsp water for 5 minutes. Drain thoroughly. **Spread** into a roasting dish and mix through 2 tbsp olive oil puréed with 3 cloves garlic. **Season** with salt and pepper. **Place** under pre-heated grill and grill for 5 minutes each side or until browned. **Place** in a mixing bowl. **Mix** through 2 tbsp lemon juice, 2 tbsp extra virgin olive oil and ¹/₂ cup finely chopped parsley. **Store** in fridge, covered with oil or wine vinegar. **Makes about 2 cups.**

## Chickpea Purée

*Make this easy purée with canned or home cooked chick peas. Use as a dip or heat as a vegetable.*

**Blend** together until smooth: 2 cups cooked chickpeas (2 cans rinsed and drained), 3 cloves chopped garlic, 2 tsp ground cumin, pinch cayenne pepper, ¹/₄ cup extra virgin oil, 1 tsp sesame oil, 1 tbsp lemon juice and salt and freshly ground black pepper to taste. **Purée** will keep 4-5 days in fridge. **Makes 2 big cups.**

## Greek Pumpkin Spread

*This is good as a spread, topping for chicken or fish, a vegetable purée to go with grills or mixed through pasta.*

**Dice** 2 cups pumpkin (500g) and drizzle over olive oil. **Cook** on high in microwave for 8 minutes or roast at 200°C until tender. **Heat** fry pan and toast 1 tsp each of fennel and cumin seeds over medium heat until they start to pop. Do not burn. **Put** ¹/₂ cup of feta cheese and all ingredients into blender. **Purée** until smooth. **Add** salt and freshly ground black pepper to taste. **Makes 3¹/₂ cups.**

## Jilly's Roasted Pepper Soup

*My friend Jilly Jardine from Queenstown is famous for her picnics. This wonderful soup is one of her favourite brews for autumn picnic expeditions. Its full rich flavour is achieved by using a mix of roasted and fresh peppers and good stock.*

**TO PREPARE:** 5 minutes    **TO COOK:** 45 minutes

**3 tbsp extra virgin olive oil**

**3 large raw red peppers,** diced

**2 medium onions,** halved and thinly sliced

**3 large roasted red peppers,** skins, seeds and pith removed, flesh diced

**1 tsp chilli paste or minced chillies**

**good pinch of cayenne**

**6 cups vegetable or chicken stock**

**1 cup fresh orange juice**

**finely grated rind of 1 orange**

**salt & freshly ground black pepper to taste**

**Optional: handful of fresh basil leaves,** torn

**Heat** oil in a large heavy soup pot over low heat.

**Add** raw peppers and onions and cook gently for 15 minutes, stirring occasionally.

**Add** diced roasted peppers, chillies, cayenne and stock.

**Bring** to the boil, then reduce heat and simmer for about 25 minutes, stirring occasionally.

**Stir** in orange juice and rind, season to taste and simmer for a further 5 minutes. Purée in batches.

**Mix** through optional torn basil leaves. Serve hot.

**Serves 4-6.**

**Variation:** garnish with wedges of avocado and strips of fried tortilla.

**Make a menu match with:** *Warm Chicken Salad with Roasted Pears and Onions.*

## Thai Pumpkin Soup

*The most time-consuming part of this recipe is cutting up the pumpkin. You can short circuit this by buying chopped pumpkin pieces in the fresh vegetable department of the supermarket. Alternatively microwave a whole pumpkin for 10 minutes to make cutting easier.*

**TO PREPARE:** 10 minutes    **TO COOK:** 30 minutes

**2 tbsp olive oil**

**1 onion,** finely chopped

**1 tbsp brown sugar**

**2 cloves garlic,** crushed

**1.2kg pumpkin** e.g. buttercup peeled and diced

**2 cups water**

**1 x 400ml can coconut milk**

**1-2 fresh or dried chillies,** finely chopped

**1 tbsp lemon grass,** minced or **½ tsp finely grated lemon rind,** no pith

**1 tbsp fish sauce**

**salt & freshly ground black pepper to taste**

**¼ cup fresh coriander or parsley,** chopped

**Heat** oil in a big pot and gently cook onion, sugar and garlic until softened (8-10 minutes).

**Add** all other ingredients except fresh coriander and simmer until tender, about 20 minutes.

**Mash,** roughly adjust seasonings to taste and mix through coriander.

**Serves 4.**

**Variation:** add prawns or diced fish for a dinner party.

**Make a menu match with:** *Greens, Pears, Spicy Pecans and Blue Cheese.*

## Ribollita – Tuscan Soup

*Zuppa de Panne – the bread soups of Tuscany are peasant dishes which use bread to enrich and thicken simple vegetable broths. Ribollita means "over boiled" so it is impossible to cook this soup too long. Vegetables can vary according to the season.*

**TO PREPARE:** 20 minutes　**TO COOK:** 2 hours 15 minutes

**Odori** (see below)

**good pinch dried chilli flakes**

**2 x 400g cans tomatoes in juice,** chopped

**2 x 310g cans beans,** e.g. 4 bean mix, rinsed and drained

**2 potatoes,** cut in chunks

**2 zucchini,** thinly sliced

**¼ red cabbage,** finely sliced

**1½ cups chicken stock** or 1 x 375ml carton

**1 litre water to cover,** more as needed

**salt & freshly ground black pepper to taste**

**4 thick slices country bread,** cut in chunks

**Optional: spinach and silverbeet,** chopped

**To finish: 2 spring onions,** finely diced; **1 tbsp fresh thyme leaves,** chopped; **extra virgin olive oil to drizzle.**

**Odori:** *Is the mixture of carrot, onion, celery and parsley which starts many Tuscan dishes. It can be made in bulk and stored for 2-3 days in refrigerator.*

**Make** Odori: heat 3 tbsp olive oil and gently cook 1 carrot, diced; 1 onion, diced; 2 stalks celery, finely diced and ½ cup chopped parsley until softened.

**Heat** Odori, chilli, tomatoes and remaining vegetables, in a big pot.

**Add** chicken stock, cover with water. Season with salt and black pepper.

**Simmer** for 2 hours if desired. Soup can be prepared a day or two ahead of time to this point and refrigerated.

**Add** bread and cook gently, stirring occasionally to prevent sticking, for a further 15 minutes. Just before serving mix in spring onions and thyme. Adjust seasoning to taste.

**Serve** each bowl with a drizzle of extra virgin olive oil.

**Serves 8-9.**

**Make a menu match with:** *Quesadillas with pesto and cheese.*

## Smoked Mussel Chowder

*Tastes creamy, but there's no cream. The combination of bacon and smoked mussels packs some great flavour. Rounded out with potatoes, celery and corn, this soup makes a satisfying, easy meal in one.*

**TO PREPARE:** 10 minutes　**TO COOK:** 30 minutes

**1 tbsp butter**

**1 large onion,** finely diced

**2 rashers bacon,** diced

**250g smoked mussels,** chopped

**1 litre water**

**3 large potatoes,** scrubbed and diced finely

**2 bay leaves**

**1 cup sweet corn**

**1 stalk celery,** finely diced

**2 cups milk**

**freshly ground black pepper to taste**

**Garnish: 2 tsp fresh thyme or tarragon,** chopped

**Heat** butter in a large pot and cook onion and bacon over medium heat until onion is softened, and bacon fat starts to run.

**Add** mussels, water, potatoes and bay leaves.

**Simmer** for 10 minutes.

**Add** sweet corn and celery and continue cooking until potatoes are tender. Lightly mash to break up potatoes.

**Add** milk, season with freshly ground black pepper and fresh thyme. Bring just to a simmer and serve.

**Serves 6.**

# A Harvester's Picnic

*Janice's Bean and Sausage Soup*

*'Carta de Musica' Sardinian Sheet Music Bread*

*Fresh Autumn Fruits*

*Greek Lemon Syrup Cake*

*Soft blue brie cheese*

## Janice's Bean and Sausage Soup

*This recipe comes from friend and neighbour Janice Sommerville, a talented and adventurous cook.*

**TO PREPARE:** 10 minutes + 12 hours soaking   **TO COOK:** 3 hours 30 minutes

**6 cups mixed dried beans** e.g. 2½ cups white; 1½ cups red kidney; ½ cup each black eyed peas, brown lentils, yellow split peas and pinto beans

**2 bacon hocks**

**16-18 cups water**

**5-6 Julia Colbasse sausages,** diced 2cm pieces

**5 x 400g cans tomatoes in juice**

**3 large onions,** peeled and diced

**8 large cloves garlic,** peeled and diced

**½ cup parsley,** preferably flat leaf, chopped

**½ cup lemon juice**

**1 tsp each ground cumin and chilli powder**

**1-2 tsp dried chilli flakes,** to taste

**salt & freshly ground black pepper to taste**

**Garnish:** ¼ cup flat leaf parsley, chopped

**Pick** through beans, removing any stones. Place in a very large pot, cover with cold water and soak for 8-12 hours.
**Boil** bacon hocks and water in a very big pot. Reduce heat to a simmer and cook for 40 minutes, skimming off scum that rises. Drain soaked beans and add to pot with diced sausage, tomatoes, onions and garlic, and simmer 2 hours more.
**Remove** hocks, and when cool remove and discard skin and shred meat.
**Add** to bean pot with parsley, lemon juice, spices, chilli flakes and season to taste.
**Simmer** another 10-15 minutes. Serve hot garnished with parsley. Soup will keep 2-3 days in fridge and freezes well.

**Serves 8-10**

**Make a menu match with:** *Garlic Pizza Bread.*

## Warm Chicken Salad with Roasted Pears and Onions

*Salads like this form a regular part of our table. It is such an easy formula–chicken spread with a little flavour paste and some onions and pears popped into the oven at the same time. Then the whole lot tossed, while still warm, through fresh salad greens with a light herb dressing.*

**TO PREPARE:** 8 minutes   **TO COOK:** 35-40 minutes

**6-8 chicken thighs,** skin removed

**1 tbsp pesto,** e.g. basil

**salt & freshly ground black pepper to taste**

**2 large red onions,** peeled, halved, cut in thin wedges

**3 big pears,** peeled, halved, cores removed and each half cut in 4 wedges

**a little oil for roasting**

**8 handfuls mixed salad greens,** washed and dried

**Pesto Dressing: 3 tbsp lemon juice; 1 tsp pesto; 3 tbsp olive oil; salt & freshly ground black pepper to taste**

**Optional Garnish: 6 slices of prosciutto**

**Preheat** oven to 200°C.
**Mix** chicken with pesto and season with salt and pepper.
**Place** on a baking dish with onions.
**Arrange** pear slices in a separate baking dish. Rub a little oil over pears to coat.
**Bake** chicken for 20-25 minutes until cooked, and pears for 35-40 minutes until golden. Allow to cool slightly.
**Combine** dressing ingredients in a jar or glass. In a large bowl toss salad leaves with dressing to coat.
**Mix** in all other ingredients. Toss gently to combine. Serve warm or at room temperature.
**Garnish:** if desired with a slice of prosciutto.

**Serves 4 as a main and 6 as a starter.**

**Make a menu match with:** *Roasted Garlic and Pumpkin Risotto.*

## Greens, Pears, Spicy Pecans and Blue Cheese

*The combination of blue cheese and pears is classic. Here wedges of juicy ripe pears combine with salad greens, spicy roasted pecan nuts and some crisp croûtons spread with soft blue cheese. The result is easy, elegant and delicious.*

**TO PREPARE:** 5 minutes    **TO COOK:** 12-15 minutes

1 tbsp oil

½ tsp each curry powder and ground cumin

1 cup pecans or fresh walnut halves

8-12 thin slices rustic country bread

2 large or 3 medium juicy pears, e.g. Comice, halved, cored, each half cut in 5-6 wedges

½ cup favourite dressing or vinaigrette

6-8 handfuls mixed salad greens, washed and dried

120g-150g soft blue cheese, e.g. Kahurangi

**Preheat** oven to 200°C.

**Mix** oil and spices through nuts in a baking dish. Bake for 10 minutes until lightly golden, taking care not to overcook. Alternatively, microwave for 3-4 minutes, stirring every minute. Reserve to one side.

**Place** bread slices in oven for 12-15 minutes to crisp. Reserve to one side. Croûtons can be made in advance and stored in an airtight container.

**Place** pear wedges in a mixing bowl and mix with dressing.

**Toss** through salad greens and toasted nuts. Divide between 4 serving plates.

**Spread** bread croûtons with cheese and serve 2 atop each salad.

**Serves 4 as a meal or 6 as a first course.**

**Variations:** lightly grill croûtons to melt cheese before garnishing salads. Use goat's cheese in place of blue cheese.

**Make a menu match with:** *Spicy Moroccan Chicken Tagine with Prunes.*

## Fruity Smoked Chicken Salad

*This combination of smoked chicken, fruit and greens with a fruity nutty dressing is one of the favourites at cooking classes I teach around the country. A range of yellow fleshed fruits can be successfully used – nectarines, mangoes and peaches. Home smoked chicken is infinitely better than store bought. For instructions on how to prepare see page 26.*

**TO PREPARE:** 10 minutes    **TO COOK:** 10 minutes

1 head of curly endive or other crisp lettuce

4 large handfuls watercress or mixed salad greens

1 recipe Fresh Walnut Dressing (see below)

2 smoked chicken breasts, sliced, or ½ smoked chicken, fat and skin removed, flesh shredded

flesh of ½ pawpaw, thinly sliced, or other yellow fruit

one small bunch of purple grapes, halved and deseeded

**Toss** greens in a large bowl with dressing to coat.

**Add** sliced cooked chicken, pawpaw and grapes and gently toss to combine.

**Pile** onto a large serving platter or 4 individual plates. Serve at once.

**Serves 4.**

**Make a menu match with:** *Salmon and Lemon Risotto.*

## Fresh Walnut Dressing

½ cup fresh walnuts or pecans or roasted cashews

¾ cup fresh orange juice

juice of ½ lemon

salt & freshly ground black pepper to taste

**Roast** nuts for dressing in a 200°C oven for 8-10 minutes or microwave for 2 minutes.

**Place** in a blender with juices and seasonings and purée until smooth and creamy. (Dressing can be made up to 2 days ahead of time and refrigerated.)

*Greens, Pears, Spicy Pecans and Blue Cheese*

## Roasted Vegetable Platter with Aïoli

*Roasted vegetables are very appealing – their flavours are so dense and rich. You can cook the vegies a day in advance and assemble this salad at your ease. If you do this, make sure you bring vegetables back to room temperature before serving.*

**TO PREPARE:** 10 minutes    **TO COOK:** 35-40 minutes

**2 medium kumara,** cut in wedges

**½ medium pumpkin,** cut in about 6-8 wedges

**2 carrots,** peeled and cut in medium batons

**1 red pepper,** cut in large chunks

**big handful of green beans**

**2 tbsp olive oil**

**2 cloves garlic,** crushed

**2 tsp fresh rosemary leaves,** chopped

**salt & freshly ground black pepper to taste**

**2 tbsp balsamic vinegar,** to toss

**Roasted Garlic Aïoli,** to accompany (see right)

**Preheat** oven to 220°C.

**Place** vegetables in a large roasting dish and mix through oil, garlic, rosemary, salt and pepper.

**Spread** out to a single layer and roast at 220°C for 35-40 minutes until starting to brown and crisp. Remove and drizzle over balsamic vinegar. Leave until warm or at room temperature.

**Pile** onto serving plates.

**Top** each with a dollop of Roasted Garlic Aïoli, Salsa Verde or Asian Pesto mixed with a little mayonnaise.

**Serves 4.**

**Make a menu match with:** *Jilly's Roasted Pepper Soup.*

## Roasted Potato Plate with Herbs and Feta Cheese

*This makes an easy stand alone dish for a vegetarian supper or weekend lunch, or serve as an accompaniment to grilled or barbecued meats.*

**TO PREPARE:** 8 minutes    **TO COOK:** 30-40 minutes

**5 large potatoes,** scrubbed, halved and cut into 3cm chunks

**2 tbsp fresh rosemary leaves,** chopped

**6 cloves garlic,** peeled and thinly sliced

**3 tbsp olive oil**

**2 tbsp balsamic vinegar**

**salt & freshly ground black pepper to taste**

**80-100g feta cheese,** sliced thinly

**Preheat** oven to 220°C.

**Place** potatoes in a large roasting dish.

**Mix** through rosemary, garlic, oil and vinegar and season with salt and pepper.

**Spread** out evenly in dish.

**Bake** for 35-40 minutes until starting to brown. Slice over feta and cook a further 5 minutes.

**Serves 2.**

**Make a menu match with:** *A crisp green salad.*

### Roasted Garlic Aïoli

*You can make aïoli, the thick yellow mayonnaise-type sauce from France with fresh or roasted garlic. Roasted garlic is smoother and has less "bite" than fresh.*

**Combine** 2 egg yolks, 3 tbsp lemon juice, 1 tsp salt, a pinch each of sugar and white pepper in a blender. With motor running add 1 cup plain oil in a slow stream, then ¼ cup extra virgin olive oil and flesh of 1 head of roasted garlic (see page 55), blending until smooth and very thick. If garlic is unroasted, follow same method using 4 fresh cloves garlic.

*Roasted Vegetable*

*Platter with Aïoli*

## Green Chilli Grits

*Grits are the American equivalent of polenta, a coarse cornmeal which cooks up to a smooth thick purée. These creamy, spicy grits take the idea of polenta into Asian/Mexican territory. They are extremely moreish. Serve with pan fried steaks and a light sauce, a wet vegetable dish like ratatouille, or even as an accompaniment to curries. Like other cornmeal dishes, if you want it porridgy you need to serve this as soon as it is made – as it cools it firms. Use it to make polenta wedges following instructions on page 49.*

**TO PREPARE:** 5 minutes   **TO COOK:** 13 minutes

**¾ cup coriander leaves,** and some soft stems

**2 green chillies,** finely chopped

**½ cup water**

**4 cups milk**

**2 shallots,** finely chopped **or 1 spring onion**

**3 garlic cloves,** finely chopped

**1 cup coarse cornmeal or quick polenta**

**salt & freshly ground black pepper to taste**

**Blend** coriander leaves, chillies and water in a food processor until they form a green purée. Put to one side.

**Heat** milk, shallots and garlic in a medium-large heavy bottomed pot and simmer gently for 4-5 minutes.

**Stir** in cornmeal in a fine stream, stirring as it is added to prevent mixture from forming lumps. Season to taste with salt and pepper.

**Reduce** heat and cook about 5-6 minutes, stirring frequently. Mixture should be thick and porridge-like.

**Stir** in coriander purée and cook for a further 1-2 minutes.

**Serve** at once.

**Serves 4.**

**Make a menu match with:** *Herb Crusted Lamb Racks or Ratatouille.*

## Provençal Ratatouille with Soft Polenta

*This is a fabulously versatile vegetable stew. You can vary the flavours by adding harissa, or pesto and olives.*

**TO PREPARE:** 7 minutes   **TO COOK:** 30 minutes

**¼ cup olive oil**

**2 large onions,** thinly sliced

**3 cloves garlic,** crushed

**1 tbsp tomato paste**

**8-10 fresh ripe tomatoes (Italian), or 2 x 400g can tomatoes in juice,** chopped

**1 tbsp dried oregano or basil**

**1 tsp honey or brown sugar**

**1 large red or yellow pepper,** diced 2-3cm

**4-5 large zucchini,** cut in thin slices

**1 medium eggplant,** diced 2-3cm

**½ cup port**

**1 tbsp spiced vinegar**

**salt & freshly ground black pepper to taste**

**Garnish: parmesan cheese, pesto**

**Polenta to accompany** (see page 49)

**Heat** oil in a big pot and cook onions over medium heat until tender but not browned (approximately 10 minutes).

**Add** garlic and tomato paste and cook a further minute.

**Mix** in all remaining ingredients, cover and simmer for 20 minutes. Adjust seasoning to taste.

**Serve** hot or at room temperature with soft or grilled polenta. Garnish each serve with shavings of parmesan cheese and a small spoon of pesto.

**Serves 6.**

**Variations:** add 400g skinless sliced chicken to vegetables in last 6-8 minutes of cooking. Or add sliced raw squid rings, diced boneless fish and prawns in last 3-4 minutes.

## Roasted Garlic and Pumpkin Risotto

*Roasted garlic is one of my mainstay flavourings over autumn and winter. I usually make up a big batch as described on page 55, as it keeps for over a month in the fridge. This is a great dish to make when it seems like the cupboard doesn't offer a lot to eat – pumpkin and parsley are the only fresh ingredients you need.*

**TO PREPARE:** 10 minutes    **TO COOK:** 25 minutes

**3 tbsp oil from roasted garlic or virgin olive oil**

**2 cups short grain Italian rice,** e.g. Carnaroli

**½ cup white wine**

**4 cups chicken stock,** hot

**2 cups pumpkin,** diced 2cm pieces

**10-12 cloves roasted garlic** (see page 55)

**½ cup fresh parmesan,** grated

**¼ cup parsley,** finely chopped

**salt & freshly ground black pepper to taste**

**Heat** oil in a heavy based pot. Add rice and stir over heat for 2 minutes.

**Add** wine and stir until evaporated.

**Add** hot stock, diced pumpkin, roasted garlic, and salt to taste and bring to a simmer. Press pumpkin into rice and cover pot. Once mixture boils reduce heat to a low simmer.

**Simmer** gently for exactly 18 minutes, stirring now and then. Rice should be sloppy.

**Mix** in parmesan and parsley. Adjust seasonings to taste, adding plenty of black pepper.

**Cover** and cook a further 2 minutes without stirring.

**Remove** from heat and stand without uncovering for 3-4 minutes before serving. If risotto looks dry, add a dash more stock.

**Serves 4 as a stand alone dish, or 6-8 as a side dish.**

**Make a menu match with:** *Herb Crusted Lamb Racks.*

## Pasta Puttanesca

*This famous dish literally translates as 'Whore's Pasta'. Back in the 50s brothels in Italy were state-owned and known as 'closed houses' because the shutters had to be kept permanently closed. The 'civil servants' of these establishments were only allowed one day a week for shopping, and with time in short supply, this sauce, made quickly from odds and ends in the pantry, became their specialty.*

**TO PREPARE:** 5 minutes    **TO COOK:** 10-12 minutes

**250g dried pasta**

**1 tbsp olive oil**

**3 cloves garlic,** crushed

**4-5 anchovy fillets,** finely chopped

**1 x 400g can tomatoes in juice,** chopped

**½ cup pitted tasty black olives,** e.g. Calamata

**pinch cayenne**

**Optional: 2 tbsp capers**

**salt & freshly ground black pepper to taste**

**2 tbsp fresh parsley,** chopped

**Cook** pasta according to manufacturer's instructions. While it cooks make the sauce.

**Heat** a large frypan with oil and gently fry garlic and anchovies over low heat until they start to sizzle.

**Add** all other ingredients except parsley, increase heat to high, and boil hard for 3-5 minutes, stirring occasionally until lightly thickened.

**Drain** pasta, return to the cooking pot and pour over the sauce. Stir over heat for a minute to combine.

**Sprinkle** with chopped parsley and serve at once.

**Serves 2. Recipe easily doubles.**

**Make a menu match with:** *A fresh green salad.*

## Pasta with Cockles and Coriander

*Large sweet cockles are available through some fish retailers. They are the closest Pacific equivalent to clams and are much sweeter than other shellfish. Mussels can be substituted. Regardless of the type of shellfish used, take great care not to overcook.*

**TO PREPARE:** 10-15 minutes    **TO COOK:** 8-10 minutes

**200-250g dried pasta**

**2 cloves of garlic,** minced

**1 tbsp olive oil**

**18-24 large fresh cockles,** cleaned **or fresh mussels,** cleaned and de-bearded

**½ cup tomato pasta sauce**

**1 cup cream**

**salt & freshly ground black pepper to taste**

**½ cup fresh coriander or parsley,** chopped

**Cook** pasta according to manufacturer's instructions.

**Heat** oil in a large pot with lid.

**Add** garlic and stir over heat until it starts to sizzle. Add cockles, cover and cook over high heat for 2-3 minutes until cockles open. Discard any which do not open.

**Remove** and de-shell ¾ of cockles, reserve some cockles in shells for garnish and reserve liquid in pot.

**Add** tomato pasta sauce and cream to reserved pan liquids. Boil for 3-4 minutes.

**Drain** pasta and mix into sauce, stir over heat 1-2 minutes to fully coat and flavour pasta.

**Mix** through shelled cockles, shell-on cockles and coriander or parsley just before serving. Cover and allow to heat through. Serve at once.

**Serves 2-3.**

**Make a menu match with:** *Mixed salad greens with Favourite Dressing.*

## Spicy Moroccan Chicken Tagine with Prunes

*A Tagine is the name given to the vessel used to cook North African stews. Over time it has come to mean the style of dish that is cooked – a slowly simmered spicy brew in this case, using dried fruits rich with spices and chilli.*

**TO PREPARE:** 10-15 minutes    **TO COOK:** 25-30 minutes

**12 chicken drumsticks or 8-10 pieces**

**½ cup lemon juice**

**2 cloves garlic,** chopped

**½ tsp turmeric or a pinch of saffron**

**2 tbsp olive oil**

**salt & freshly ground black pepper to taste**

**2 onions,** peeled, halved and thinly sliced

**2 chillies,** minced

**1 tbsp each ground cumin and ground coriander**

**4 cardamom pods or 1 tsp crushed cardamom seeds**

**1 tsp each ground ginger and turmeric**

**3 cups water**

**1 cup dried pitted prunes, or dried apricots**

**½ cup fruit chutney,** e.g. peach or mango

**Marinate** chicken in a non-reactive bowl or clean plastic bag with lemon juice, garlic and turmeric or saffron for 1-2 hours turning occasionally. Remove chicken, season with salt and pepper and reserve marinade.

**Heat** oil in a large heavy ovenproof pan or pot. Brown chicken well all over. Lift chicken out of pan and put to one side.

**Add** onions and all spices to pan and cook gently for 5-6 minutes. Mix in reserved marinade, water and prunes, bring to a boil then reduce heat and simmer 15 minutes.

**Add** chicken back into pan and mix in chutney. Cover and cook over low heat for 30-40 minutes until very tender. Alternately bake covered at 180°C for 40-45 minutes. Adjust seasonings to taste.

**Serves 6.**

# The First Fire

*Chicken, Bacon, Garlic and Mushroom Pies*

*Lightly cooked green beans or zucchini*

*Fruit Crumble with Ginger, Cardamom and Cashews*

*cheese platter*

# Chicken, Bacon, Garlic and Mushroom Pies

*Based on a classic French Coq au Vin (chicken in wine) with a pastry crust, this is a really easy way to make pies. The chicken mixture simmers in a pot. The individual pastry squares cook in the oven and when you are ready to serve simply spoon the hot filling into the split pastries.*

**TO PREPARE:** 15 minutes    **TO COOK:** 40-45 minutes

**2 tbsp olive oil**

**400g button mushrooms,** wiped with damp cloth

**3 rashers bacon,** diced

**8-10 baby onions,** peeled and halved

**12 cloves garlic,** peeled and halved

**1 x 400g can tomatoes in juice,** chopped

**1½ cups red wine**

**3 cups chicken stock** or 2 x 375ml cartons

**3 bay leaves**

**1 tsp fresh rosemary,** chopped

**2 tsp fresh thyme,** chopped

**salt & freshly ground black pepper to taste**

**800g boneless, skinless chicken thighs,** quartered

**3 tbsp cornflour**

**2 tbsp port or sherry**

**2-3 sheets puff pastry**

**1 egg beaten, or a little milk**

**Heat** oil in a large heavy pot.

**Add** mushrooms and bacon. Brown well, then remove and put to one side.

**Add** onions and garlic to pot and cook gently for 8-10 minutes until onion is softened and starting to brown.

**Add** tomatoes and juice, wine, stock, herbs and seasonings, browned mushrooms and bacon to the pot.

**Simmer** gently for 20 minutes. Sauce can be prepared ahead of time to this point.

**Add** chicken and bring sauce back to a simmer. Cover and simmer gently 8-10 minutes until chicken is cooked through.

**Combine** cornflour and port or sherry and mix into sauce, stirring over heat until lightly thickened.

**Adjust** seasonings to taste.

**Cut** each sheet of pastry in quarters. If desired garnish each square with pastry cut outs. Place on a baking tray and brush with egg or milk.

**Bake** at 220°C for 8-10 minutes then reduce to 180°C and cook a further 10 minutes or until pastry is puffed, golden and cooked through.

**To assemble pies:** split each cooked pastry in half through the middle, spoon over hot chicken filling and place pastry lid on top.

**Serves 6-8.**

**Variation:** chicken pie can also be cooked in the oven. Prepare sauce, thicken and cool. Mix with raw chicken, place in a pie dish, cover with pastry and bake at 200°C for 30-35 minutes.

**Make a menu match with:** *Lightly cooked green beans.*

---

**PERFECT RICE**

*Wash rice well under cold running water. Place in a pot with cold water at ratio of 1½ cups water per cup of rice. Add 1 tsp salt. Bring to a boil over high heat, then cover tightly. Reduce heat to lowest setting and cook for 15 minutes. Remove from heat without uncovering and stand a further 15 minutes. Fluff up with a fork and serve.*

## Spice Seared Lamb with Chickpea Purée and Eggplant

*Here's one for carnivores. Any quick cooking lamb cut, such as lamb racks, rumps or lamb fillets, works well in this great autumn combination. Remember to rest meat for about 5 minutes before slicing. This allows the juices to disperse evenly.*

**TO PREPARE:** 10 minutes    **TO COOK:** 15-20 minutes

**1-2 lamb rumps or 4 lamb fillets**

**1-2 tsp Cajun spice mix,** to taste

**salt & freshly ground black pepper to taste**

**2 tbsp olive oil**

**2 tsp pesto**

**1 medium eggplant,** cut 2cm thick slices

**¾ cup Chickpea Purée,** heated (see page 33)

**Sauce: 1 tsp tomato paste; ¼ cup stock; 1 tbsp port; 1 tsp balsamic vinegar; pinch sugar; salt & freshly ground black pepper to taste.**

**Preheat** oven to 220°C. Rub lamb all over with spice mix. Season with salt and pepper. Heat 1 tsp of olive oil in a heavy pan and brown lamb well all over (5 minutes). Transfer to a small roasting dish.

**Mix** rest of olive oil with pesto and brush on both sides of each slice of eggplant. Arrange slices in a single layer on a baking tray. Season with salt and pepper. Place eggplant in hot oven and cook for 10-12 minutes.

**Add** lamb to oven and bake for 6-8 minutes until lamb is medium rare, and eggplant is lightly golden.

**Rest** lamb and eggplant for 5 minutes. While it rests make sauce and heat Chickpea Purée.

**Heat** pan used to brown meat. Fry tomato paste for 1 minute. Add stock, port, vinegar and sugar and simmer 2-3 minutes. Season to taste with salt and pepper.

**Slice** each rump in half, then each half into 4-5 slices. Fan meat onto 2 heated serving plates.

**Layer** eggplant slices alongside, spooning a little Chickpea Purée between each. Spoon sauce over and around meat.

**Serves 2. Recipe easily doubles.**

**Make a menu match with:** *Impeccably fresh oysters to start and Manhattan Lime Meringue Tart to finish.*

## Roasted Snapper with Ginger Tamarind Crust

*This is one of my favourite ways to use tamarind – don't attempt the recipe without it. Roasting is an easy moist way to cook a whole fish and works well with fish up to about 2kg in weight. The ginger paste also works well with chicken.*

**TO PREPARE:** 5 minutes    **TO COOK:** 10-20 minutes

**1 whole very fresh fish 1kg-2kg, e.g. snapper or 1 side salmon**

**Ginger Tamarind Paste: 4cm piece fresh ginger,** peeled and grated (needs to be soft fresh ginger); **2 fresh lemon or lime leaves,** minced; **2 tsp tamarind pulp; 1 tbsp oil; ½ tsp salt;** freshly ground black pepper.

**Use** a sharp knife to slash a diamond pattern on both sides of whole fish. If using a side of salmon, leave skin on and remove the pin bones.

**Purée** all paste ingredients together. Rub into whole fish working marinade into cuts. If using a side of salmon spread paste over the skinless side.

**Place** fish in fridge for ½ hour or up to 8 hours.

**Preheat** oven to 250°C.

**Bake** fish for 10-20 minutes – for whole fish, cook until eye starts to whiten and cuts start to open up. For a side of fish e.g. salmon, cook just until fish gives when pressed in the deepest part and a little white juice forms beads on the top. Take care not to overcook. Stand for 3-4 minutes before serving.

**Serves 4.**

**Make a menu match with:** *Perfect rice and a green salad.*

*Cornmeal Polenta & Semolina.* *At its most basic, polenta is a porridge made with coarse cornmeal and water. Usually salt, pepper, parmesan cheese and a little butter are added to round out the flavour. But this need not be the case – the blandness of this useful starch makes it ideal for other flavour diversions – the recipe for Green Chilli Grits on page 42 takes polenta into new Asian/Mexican territory. When first cooked polenta is smooth, creamy and very soothing. At this stage it makes the perfect foil for wet dishes like casseroles, curries and vegetable dishes like ratatouille. Leave it to cool and polenta gets firm – trying to reheat it back to a creamy texture is not a good look. Firm polenta can be sliced and grilled or fried and is then ready for all manner of sophisticated little toppings – pan cooked mushrooms with garlic, lemon and fresh herbs (or try the Mushroom Sauce served with Sausages on page 66), some fresh goat's cheese or blue cheese melted over the top or a little roasted tomato Topping – the possibilities are endless.*

## Soft Polenta

*If you have a choice use 5 minute polenta; it is just so much easier than all that stirring.*

**Follow** manufacturer's instructions for cooking polenta – coarse cornmeal usually takes longer than fine. Take care to add cornmeal in a thin stream stirring all the time, to prevent mix from clumping. **Add** 1 tsp salt per cup of cornmeal. **Mix** in 1 tbsp butter and $1/4$ cup grated parmesan cheese once thickened, or flavour with other things such as pesto, olive paste, Harissa, blue cheese or roasted garlic. **Serve** at once – the mixture should be thick like porridge. **Serves 4.**

## Grilled Polenta Wedges

*Using the cooked polenta as a base, put the mixture into a shallow greased dish, spread out evenly and allow to cool. Cut into shapes and either fry, grill or barbecue. Top with any of your favourite flavours. Serve small polenta wedges as a pre-dinner or party nibble with a little blue cheese or goat's cheese grilled on the top. Make polenta wedges using plain polenta or flavour with other ingredients – as for soft polenta.*

**Serves 4-6.**

## Basic Savoury Semolina

*For the lazy cook, semolina makes a really good substitute for soft polenta – the texture is finer and although it is made with wheat not cornmeal, a similar result is achieved with much less effort.*

**Heat** 3 cups milk and 50g butter in a heavy pot. **Add** $1^{1}/4$ cups semolina, 1 tsp salt, a pinch nutmeg and some freshly ground black pepper. **Stir** over heat until it boils and thickens. Simmer for 3-4 minutes. **Remove** from heat and mix in $1/2$ cup freshly grated parmesan cheese. **Serve** at once or use as the basis for a range of savoury bakes. **Serves 4-6.**

## Savoury Baked Semolina Slice

*This is a great recipe for an easy lunch or supper. It even tastes good cold, and like other polenta styled dishes, lends itself well to all sorts of flavour adaptations.*

**Prepare** basic savoury semolina. **Mix** in 2 eggs, and 1 cup grated cheddar cheese, plus flavourings of your choice such as chopped bacon, corn, peppers, pesto etc. **Spoon** into a greased baking dish and bake at 200°C for 20- 25 minutes until puffed and golden. Serve hot or at room temperature – it will deflate a little as it cools but still tastes great. **Serves 4-6.**

# Quesadillas

*It's easy to get excited by the creative possibilities of fresh tortillas – as a carbohydrate base they are fabulously versatile. In recent years tortillas, be they flour or cornmeal, have taken on numerous innovative interpretations under the hands of the new chefs, who use them to create salads and salad baskets, sweet crunchy crispbreads, canapé bases, wrappers for grilled and roasted meats and as a thickening for soups and sauces.*

*Of all their re-inventions, those of the quesadilla, pronounced 'kay-sa-dee-yaa', offer the greatest scope for the home cook. Traditionally a tortilla turnover, quesadillas are the Mexican equivalent of pizza, and as such, are open to a raft of creative interpretations. In their most basic form, quesadillas are made by sprinkling some chillies and/or cheese onto half a tortilla, which is then folded over and fried on both sides; sometimes refried beans are added. Take them into today's kitchen with adventurous filling combinations for a great snack or supper, or an accompaniment to soups or salads.*

*Quesadillas can be cooked in a pan or in the oven:*

**To pan cook,** cover one side of a tortilla with filling ingredients, fold over other half of tortilla to cover and fry in a heated pan on both sides until starting to puff and brown.

**To bake**, sandwich the filling between 2 whole tortillas, place on a baking tray and bake at 200°C for 8-10 minutes. Cut in wedges to serve.

## Some Yummy Quesadilla Combinations:

*Pesto, smoked salmon slices and brie.*

*Smoked chicken, gruyère and red pepper.*

*Olive paste, sliced tomatoes and feta.*

*Pesto, peppers, parmesan and olives.*

*Spicy sausage, cheddar and roasted peppers.*

*Curried chicken, fresh coriander and mozzarella.*

*Spinach, brie and toasted pine nuts.*

*Ratatouille, olives and raclette.*

*Mozzarella, parma ham and fresh basil leaves.*

*Harissa and grated cheese.*

*Melted chocolate and sliced banana.*

*Banana and cinnamon sugar.*

## Cheat's Lavosh

*This is a great shortcut to make crisp thin lavosh-like flatbreads. Once made, they will keep for several weeks in an airtight container in a cool place and can be refreshed in a hot oven for 3-4 minutes.*

**Cut** fresh tortillas into long thin wedges. **Brush** one side of each wedge with beaten egg. **Sprinkle** egg side generously with poppy seeds or sesame seeds. **Place** on a baking tray and bake at 200°C for 10-12 minutes until crisp. Store in an airtight container.

## Crispy Tortilla Salad Baskets

*Yes, you can make them with fresh tortillas and don't need to fry them. You need two heatproof pudding bowls as moulds.*

**Preheat** oven to 200°C. **Place** a fresh tortilla in a pudding bowl, folding to follow bowl shape. **Stack** another bowl on top to secure. **Place** on a baking tray and bake for 10 minutes, then remove from mould and bake a further 10 minutes until crisp.

# Winter

**Winter's bareness has its own rewards.**

**Sharing stories around a fire**

**over a bowl of rib sticking black bean soup,**

the comfort of mashed potatoes and sausages, weekend dress up dinner parties with giant hearty cassoulets or spicy tagines.

Our cocooning season is given over to good conversation and hearty, warming, but never stodgy food. We eat roots – mashed, roasted, puréed into soups, and simmered with meats for a tasty Pot-au-feu. Harissa and Asian Pesto bring flavours afresh to winter plates. Asian greens with their riveting freshness come to the fore – stir fried with a dash of oil and water and splashed with oyster sauce, cooked in rich noodle broths with roasted duck and orange rinds – the temper for our rich winter meats. The inclemency of the weather might keep us indoors but it does make us feel good about being in the kitchen – cooking, eating and sharing food with others – food that is comfortable, nurturing and rich with the flavours of gentle slow cooking.

*Brazilian Black Bean Soup, page 58*

**W**inter is one time we all need a little help. With the growing season in hibernation, it is easy for food to become monotonous and dull. Enter a range of flavours to bring new zing to winter tastes. Use them in casseroles, dressings, sauces and soups.

## Harissa

*From the heart of North African cooking comes this spicy red hot paste. Use judiciously to uplift soups, stews and sauces. Its fiery lift adds wonderful richness. Once you have made harissa you'll find it an indispensable kitchen flavouring.*

**Heat** a frypan, and dry toast 2 tsp coriander seeds and 1 tsp caraway seeds over a medium heat until they start to crackle and pop – don't let them burn. **Remove** and add 1 tsp cayenne and 1 tsp ground cumin. **Grind** together in a mortar and pestle or spice grinder. **Heat** 2 tbsp oil and gently fry 4 cloves crushed garlic and 1 tbsp chilli flakes for 1-2 minutes. **Remove** from heat and place in blender with flesh of 2 roasted red peppers or 1 cup tomato purée and ground spices. **Purée** until smooth. **Spoon** into a jar, cover with a layer of oil and refrigerate. **Makes about 1¼ cups.** Harissa will keep for 2-3 weeks in the fridge.

## Asian Pesto

*Use landcress or watercress to make this indispensable pesto. Boiling water fixes the colour of the herbs, and prevents them from oxidising.*

**Wash** a big bunch of cress and a whole coriander plant and remove and discard tough stems. **Place** in a heatproof bowl and pour over boiling water to cover. **Drain** at once. **Place** in a blender with 2 cloves garlic, peeled, 2 small chillies, de-stemmed, ¼ cup roasted peanuts or roasted cashew nuts and ¼ cup salad oil. **Purée** all together until the mixture forms a smooth paste. Pesto will keep for 10-12 days in fridge, with a layer of oil on the top. **Makes 1 cup.**

### Winter Mint and Parsley Pesto

*The fresh clean flavour of this pesto goes well with classic tastes – it's a great boost for winter flavours.*

**Purée** together until smooth 1 large bunch of parsley without stalks, 2-3 cloves peeled garlic, $1/4$ cup freshly grated parmesan cheese, 2 tbsp toasted pinenuts or walnuts and $1/2$ cup olive oil. **Season** with salt and freshly ground black pepper to taste. Keeps 2 weeks in the fridge, covered with a layer of oil on top. **Makes about 1½ cups.**

### Roasted Garlic

*The flavour of roasted garlic is incredibly sweet and smooth. Cook up 3 or 4 whole heads of garlic at a time for a standby lift to pastas, sauces and soups. In this easy method, the garlic is first peeled and then baked in olive oil – no mess, no waste. Whole heads of garlic can be cooked by the same method.*

Per whole head of garlic, allow $1/4$ cup olive oil. **Preheat** oven to 150°C. **Peel** garlic cloves and place in an ovenproof container. **Pour** over oil. **Cover** and bake for 45-50 minutes until garlic is very soft. Cool. **Pour** oil and garlic into a container and store in fridge. It will keep for weeks.

### Lemons and Limes Pickled in Oil

*These lemons and limes are great for winter hot pots, tagines and braises and make a useful condiment for grills and barbecues. To use, discard pulp and slice rinds finely.*

**Wash** 6 lemons and limes and cut into thin wedges. **Freeze** until firm. **Sprinkle** over 6 tbsp coarse salt. **Leave** for about an hour. **Layer** slices into sterilised jars and pour on any brine that has collected on the plate. **Sprinkle** paprika between the layers, and tuck a bay leaf in the top.

**Cover** with soya or salad oil. They will keep 2-3 months. **Makes about 1 large jar.**

## Brazilian Black Bean Soup

*In the early 80s I spent the best part of a year in Brazil, in the little town of Buzios, about an hour and a half north of Rio de Janeiro. Black beans were the daily staple – usually served simply boiled with rice, or for special occasions brewed up into a complex feijoada. Here they form a fabulously easy and delicious soup – great for a Sunday lunch with friends or to fill the fridge for a busy week ahead. Best of all there's no presoaking needed for the beans. You'll need a big pot.*

**TO PREPARE:** 5 minutes    **TO COOK:** 2 hours 15 minutes

**4 cups dried black beans**

**16 cups water,** or more as needed

**500g piece boiling bacon or 2 bacon hocks**

**6 cloves garlic,** peeled and crushed

**2 tsp ground cumin**

**2 cups tomato pasta sauce**

**2 tbsp hot chilli sauce,** to taste

**salt & freshly ground black pepper to taste**

**½ cup fresh coriander or parsley,** chopped

**Optional garnish: mild red chillies,** thinly sliced and lightly fried in a little oil

**Wash,** drain and rinse beans. Place beans in a pot with water, bacon or hocks, garlic, cumin, tomato pasta sauce and chilli sauce.

**Bring** to the boil, removing any scum that rises.

**Simmer** on lowest heat uncovered for 2 hours – once fully cooked, soup should be lightly thickened. Take care during last half hour of cooking that soup does not catch.

**Remove** bacon, and cut into small chunks, discarding skin and fat if using hocks. Return pieces to soup pot.

**Season** to taste, with 1-2 tsp salt and plenty of freshly ground black pepper. Mix in coriander. If desired garnish with red chillies which have been lightly fried.

**Serves 8-10.**

**Make a menu match with:** *Naan Bread.*

## Spicy Thai Seafood Soup

*This is one of those great store cupboard dinners that needs only the addition of fresh seafood to make a hearty meal. If you are feeling rich you can use prawns and fresh fish fillets; if you are feeling poor make it with mussels.*

**TO PREPARE:** 10 minutes    **TO COOK:** 25 minutes

**1 tbsp oil**

**1 large onion,** finely diced

**1 tsp each crushed garlic and fresh root ginger**

**2 tbsp Thai curry paste,** to taste

**1 x 400ml can coconut cream**

**1 x 375ml carton fish stock,** made up to 2 cups with water

**400g mixed fresh seafoods,** cut into bite-sized pieces

**salt & freshly ground black pepper to taste**

**2 tbsp fresh coriander,** chopped

**Heat** oil in a large pot and cook the onion over gentle heat until softened.

**Add** garlic, ginger and curry paste and stir over heat for a minute.

**Add** coconut cream, and stock with water. Simmer for 10 minutes. Sauce can be prepared ahead of time to this point.

**Add** fresh seafood, season to taste with salt and freshly ground black pepper and cook over very low heat for 3-4 minutes until seafood is cooked.

**Mix** in the coriander just before serving.

**Serves 4.**

**Make a menu match with:** *Greens, Pears, Spicy Pecans and Blue Cheese.*

## Pea and Ham Soup

*Infinitely nourishing and satisfying this thick rustic soup fends off the bleakest days of winter. You can make it with green or yellow split peas; either way it's rib sticking stuff.*

**TO PREPARE:** 5 minutes     **TO COOK:** 2 hours 45 minutes

**1 bacon hock or some bacon bones and 225g**

**boiling bacon in one piece**

**16 cups water**

**2 bay leaves**

**1½ cups chicken stock** or 1 x 375ml carton

**2 onions,** peeled and finely diced

**6 sprigs fresh mint**

**3 cups dried split peas**

**salt & freshly ground black pepper to taste**

**Optional: 2-3 tbsp Winter Mint and Parsley Pesto**

**or Harissa** (see pages 54 and 55)

**Place** hock, water, bay leaves and stock in a large pot.
**Bring** to the boil, removing any scum that rises to the surface.
**Add** onions and mint, reduce heat to a low simmer. Cook gently for 1½ hours.
**Add** peas and simmer gently for 1 hour until thick, taking care soup does not catch on the bottom of the pot.
**Remove** mint sprigs and bay leaves and discard.
**Lift** bacon hock from soup and when cool enough to handle, remove skin and any fat and discard.
**Shred** meat. Add back into soup. Bring back to a simmer.
**Season** with salt and freshly ground black pepper to taste. Reheat to serve.
**Mix** through optional pesto or harissa. Soup will keep in the fridge for up to 5 days.

**Serves 8-10.**

**Make a menu match with:** *Warm Chicken Salad with Roasted Pears and Onions.*

## Chicken and Kumara Soup with Asian Pesto

*Taking a tangent on the classic leek and potato soup, this easy brew uses a whole chicken for a substantial meal in one. Skin the chicken before cooking to reduce fat.*

**TO PREPARE:** 20 minutes     **TO COOK:** 2 hours

**1 whole fresh chicken,** skin and visible fat removed

**12 cups water**

**8 cloves garlic,** peeled

**1 onion,** diced

**2 bay leaves**

**3 sprigs fresh thyme**

**2 tsp curry powder,** fried 1 minute in hot dry pan or microwaved 1 minute to release flavours

**2 medium kumara,** peeled and diced

**4 medium floury potatoes,** peeled and diced

**2 leeks,** washed and sliced in thin rounds

**2 cups corn kernels**

**salt & freshly ground black pepper to taste**

**Garnish:** ½ cup Asian Pesto

**Place** chicken in a big pot with water, bring to a simmer, removing any scum that rises.
**Add** garlic, onion, herbs and fried curry powder and simmer very gently for 1 hour.
**Lift** chicken out of pot and allow to cool. Discard bay leaves and thyme sprigs.
**Add** kumara, potatoes and leeks to pot and simmer 40 minutes. Lightly mash to break up potatoes.
**Add** corn and flesh of cooked chicken, bring back to a simmer and season with salt and pepper to taste.
**Mix** through pesto or serve each bowl with a dollop of pesto.

**Serves 8-10.**

**Make a menu match with:** *'Carta de Musica' Sardinian Sheet Music Bread and Greek Lemon Syrup Cake.*

## El Paso Chicken and Vegetable Soup

*Combining a piece of tender moist chicken on the bone with root vegetables in a spicy chicken broth, this soup makes a satisfying and stylish dish to beat the cold.*

**TO PREPARE:** 15 minutes    **TO COOK:** 20 minutes

**8 cups well-flavoured chicken stock**

**6 chicken quarters or chicken supremes**

**½ buttercup pumpkin (600-800g),** peeled and cut in large 4cm chunks

**3 medium potatoes,** peeled and cut in large 4cm chunks

**small bunch baby carrots,** trimmed, **or 2 carrots cut in thin strips**

**3 corn cobs,** cut into 2cm rounds

**salt & freshly ground black pepper to taste**

**2-3 tomatoes,** peeled, cores removed, flesh cut in eighths

**1-2 fresh chillies,** very finely chopped

**2 spring onions,** very finely chopped

**2-3 tbsp Asian Pesto or Winter Mint and Parsley Pesto** (see pages 54 and 55)

**½ packed cup fresh coriander,** chopped

**Bring** chicken stock to a simmer in a large pot, seasoning to taste with salt and pepper.

**Add** chicken, pumpkin, potatoes, carrots and corn, season with salt and pepper, cover and simmer for 12-15 minutes until chicken and vegetables are cooked.

**Season** to taste and mix in tomatoes, chillies, spring onions and pesto just prior to serving. Bring back to a simmer.

**To serve,** place a portion of chicken into six deep bowls. Spoon over vegetables and ladle over broth.

**Serves 6.**

**Make a menu match with:** *Naan Bread or Quesadillas.*

## Classic Country Lamb, Barley and Vegetable Soup

*This would have to be one of New Zealand's classics – generations have been nurtured on its soothing flavours. As children, it was the mainstay of after school winter sustenance. For a kick, finish it off with a good dollop of Harissa, or some Winter Mint and Parsley Pesto.*

**TO PREPARE:** 15 minutes    **TO COOK:** 2 hours

**4 lamb shanks,** trimmed of any fat

**2 cups pearl barley or dried soup mix**

**3 bay leaves**

**16 cups water**

**salt & freshly ground black pepper to taste**

**3 cups each of grated carrots and kumara, or pumpkin**

**2 onions,** finely diced

**4 stalks celery,** finely chopped

**¼ cup tomato paste**

**1 x 400g can tomatoes in juice,** roughly chopped

**Optional garnish:** 2-3 tbsp Harissa or Winter Parsley Pesto

**Place** all ingredients in large pot, except for garnish.

**Bring** to a boil, removing any scum as it rises.

**Reduce** heat to a simmer. Cook gently for 2 hours.

**Lift** shanks from soup. When cool enough to handle strip off meat and shred.

**Remove** any fat from top of soup.

**Return** shredded meat back to soup. Season to taste and bring back to a simmer. Serve hot, topping each bowl, if desired, with a small dollop of Harissa or Pesto.

**Makes** 18 cups. Soup will keep in the fridge for 4-5 days and freezes well.

**Serves 12.**

**Make a menu match with:** *'Carta de Musica' Sardinian Sheet Music Bread and a platter of blue cheese and pears.*

# Lunch on a Wet Sunday

El Paso Chicken and Vegetable Soup

Cheese and Chilli Quesadillas

Salad of Roasted Root Vegetables

90s Tarte Tatin

## Pacific Pot-au-feu – A Boil Up

*The French have long glamourised their boil ups through the simple use of the term pot-au-feu. What is a pot-au-feu? A pot on the fire, simmered with meat and vegies until they are melt in the mouth tender. Every nationality has their version of a 'Boil Up'. This one is classic Kiwi. Any leftover meat makes great sandwiches.*

**TO PREPARE:** 10 minutes    **TO COOK:** 2 hours 15 minutes

**1 piece pickled pork** (1-1.3kg)

**2 bunches puha or watercress,** washed

**3-4 medium kumara,** peeled and cut 4cm chunks

**4-6 medium potatoes,** peeled and cut 4cm chunks

**600-800g pumpkin,** peeled & cut into 4cm chunks

**salt & freshly ground black pepper to taste**

**½ cup Asian Pesto** (see page 54)

**Place** pickled pork in a pot with enough water to cover. Bring to a boil and then reduce heat to a simmer.

**Simmer** for 1 hour, removing any scum as it rises.

**Wash** greens under tap; if using puha, rub hard under running water until fibres break and water runs green – this removes bitter, milky sap.

**Add** greens to pork and simmer gently for another hour.

**Boil** potatoes, pumpkin and kumara in a separate pot of lightly salted water until just tender.

**To serve,** lift pork from pot. Slice thinly, return to pot with cooked vegetables. Bring to a simmer.

**Ladle** meat and vegetables into deep bowls, spoon over a little cooking broth, dollop a big spoonful of Asian Pesto on top and serve with crusty bread.

**Serves 4-6. Recipe is easily extended.**

**Variation:** use fresh pork, and add a can of coconut milk and some Harissa to the broth.

**Make a menu match with:** *Naan Bread.*

## Chinese Roast Duck Noodle Soup

*Count your luck if you have ready access to freshly roasted Chinese ducks. Serve the duck in chunks on the bone or de-bone and de-skin for a more elegant and lower fat version.*

**TO PREPARE:** 10 minutes    **TO COOK:** 25 minutes

**½ roasted Chinese duck** (Get the duck man to chop in small pieces. If you wish to remove skin and fat you can leave the duck in one piece)

**3 cups chicken stock** or 2 x 375ml cartons

**3 cups water**

**3 long thick strips of orange rind,** cut with a peeler

**2 tsp root ginger,** grated

**2 tbsp oyster sauce**

**4 "nests" dried Chinese egg noodles** (250g)

**2 heads baby bok choy,** washed and cut lengthwise in quarters

**1 spring onion,** finely sliced

**handful fresh coriander leaves**

**Place** duck in a pot, pour over stock and water, add orange rind, ginger and oyster sauce.

**Bring** to a simmer, cover.

**Cook** for 20 minutes. Skim off fat.

**Lift** out duck from soup, deskin, defat, and debone if desired. Strip off meat and shred into bite-sized pieces (or leave in pieces on the bone). Thinly slice the orange rind.

**Add** noodles to broth and cook according to manufacturer's instructions.

**Add** cooked duck meat back into the pot along with sliced orange rind, bok choy, spring onions and coriander, two minutes before noodles are ready.

**Simmer** 2 minutes and serve at once.

**Serves 4 as a meal. Recipe doubles easily.**

**Make a menu match with:** *Naan Bread.*

*Chinese Roast Duck Noodle Soup*

## Roasted Walnut, Orange and Beet Salad

*This pretty salad makes a great accompaniment to a winter casserole or main course dish. Re-work it as a stand alone meal by incorporating some lightly pan fried lamb fillets – cook them to medium rare then thinly slice and toss through the salad with other ingredients.*

**TO PREPARE:** 10 minutes    **TO COOK:** 6-8 minutes

**³/₄ cup walnuts**

**8 handfuls mixed salad greens,** washed and dried

**2 oranges,** peeled and flesh cut in segments

**1 beetroot,** peeled and cut in matchstick strips

**¹/₂ cup favourite dressing,** with finely grated rind of ¹/₂ orange added

**Roast** walnuts in a 200°C oven in a shallow dish for 6-8 minutes, or gently fry in a little oil for 2-3 minutes.
**Prepare** salad ingredients.
**Toss** greens with dressing in a big bowl then toss through with all other salad ingredients.
**Pile** onto 4 serving plates.

**Serves 4.**

## For Salad with Lamb Fillets

**Heat** a frypan with a little oil. **Season** 4-6 lamb fillets with salt and freshly ground black pepper. Cook over medium-high heat for 3-4 minutes, until medium rare.
**Stand** 3-5 minutes then slice fillets on an angle, 2cm thick.
**Toss** through salad with all other ingredients. Accompany with flatbread.

## Salad of Bitter Greens and Grapefruit

*Here's another great wintery accompaniment salad that can be extended to a main course role with the addition of some chicken – the home smoked chicken on page 26 is superb.*

**TO PREPARE:** 5 minutes

**1 head curly endive or other bitter greens**

**1 large bunch watercress,** stems removed

**2 large grapefruit,** peeled and segmented

**Optional: flesh of 1 large avocado,** sliced

**¹/₂ cup favourite vinaigrette**

**Wash** and dry salad greens. Place in a large bowl.
**Use** 2 large spoons to toss with dressing then gently toss through all other ingredients and divide amongst 6 serving plates. Serve at once.

**Serves 6.**

**Make a menu match with:** *Black Bean Soup.*

## Favourite Dressing for Greens

**1 egg yolk**

**¹/₃ cup soya or salad oil**

**2 tbsp red or white wine vinegar**

**1 tsp Dijon mustard**

**salt & freshly ground black pepper to taste**

**1 tsp brown sugar**

**juice of ¹/₂ lemon**

**Mix** all together. Keep chilled and use within 24 hours of making.

**Makes about ¹/₂ cup. Recipe easily doubles or trebles.**

## Pumpkin, Spinach and Goat's Cheese Lasagne

*You can assemble this a day ahead of time and refrigerate ready to cook up. Even the meat lovers like it.*

**TO PREPARE:** 30 minutes   **TO COOK:** 30 minutes

**2 bunches fresh spinach** (or 250g frozen)

**2 tbsp pesto**

**3 cups pumpkin,** cooked, drained and mashed

**2 cloves garlic,** crushed

**100g ricotta or cottage cheese,** mixed with

**150g goat's cheese or feta,** finely crumbled

**½ tsp fresh nutmeg,** grated

**2 eggs**

**salt & freshly ground black pepper to taste**

**2 cups pasta tomato sauce,** mixed with 1 cup water

**3 fresh lasagne sheets,** cut 25cm x 40cm (250g pack)

**1 cup grated cheese,** e.g. cheddar

**Wash** spinach, then drop into a pot of boiling water for 30 seconds. Drain under cold water and squeeze out all moisture. (If using frozen spinach, thaw and then squeeze dry). Roughly chop, mix through pesto and season to taste with salt and pepper.

**Mix** mashed pumpkin with garlic, cottage cheese, feta, nutmeg and eggs. Season to taste with salt and pepper.

**Spread** 1 cup of pasta sauce/water mix into the base of a 22cm x 33cm baking dish.

**Cover** with a layer of lasagne sheets. Spread over spinach, top with another layer of lasagne. Spread with pumpkin and cheese mixture, then a final layer of lasagne.

**Pour** over the rest of the pasta sauce, spreading evenly. Sprinkle top with cheese.

**Bake** uncovered at 180°C for 20 minutes.

**Place** under grill to brown top if desired.

**Serves 6.**

**Make a menu match with:** *Winter salad greens.*

## Pasta with Asian Pesto and Roasted Pumpkin

*Al dente pasta tossed with a spicy cress pesto and sweet densely flavoured roasted pumpkin. Try other types of pesto for a flavour variation.*

**TO PREPARE:** 10 minutes   **TO COOK:** 30 minutes

**400g pumpkin,** peeled, de-seeded and cut into 2cm pieces

**2 tbsp olive oil**

**1 tsp fresh rosemary,** chopped

**salt & freshly ground black pepper to taste**

**200g dried fusilli,** or pasta tubes

**½ cup Asian Pesto** (see page 55)

**Garnish: parmesan cheese**

**Preheat** oven to 220°C.

**Place** pumpkin in a roasting dish, mix through oil and rosemary, season with salt and pepper.

**Roast** for 30 minutes until lightly golden, stirring once.

**Cook** pasta according to manufacturer's instructions, while pumpkin roasts.

**Drain** pasta, toss through pesto and roasted pumpkin.

**Shave** over parmesan cheese to garnish.

**Serves 2. Recipe easily doubles.**

**Make a menu match with:** *Fruit Crumble with Ginger Cardamom and Cashews.*

### GREMOLATA

**Another** versatile seasoning for winter, gremolata combines freshly chopped parsley, garlic and lemon, usually in the ratio of ½ cup chopped parsley, 2 cloves minced garlic and 2 tsp finely chopped lemon rind (no pith). **Preserved** lemon rind makes an interesting substitute for fresh rinds. **Sprinkle** gremolata over stews, soups and casseroles. Stored in the fridge it will keep 1-2 days. **Makes ½ cup.**

*Fettucine Carbonara with Spinach and Broccoli*

## Fettucine Carbonara with Spinach and Broccoli

*A great one-dish dinner that delivers the prescribed fix of antioxidant vegetables in a thoroughly delicious way.*

**TO PREPARE:** 10-12 minutes   **TO COOK:** 10-12 minutes

**250g dried spaghetti**

**1 tbsp olive oil**

**2-3 rashers bacon,** diced

**1 large clove garlic,** crushed

**2-3 heads spinach,** stalks removed, leaves washed and roughly chopped, left wet

**1 head broccoli,** cut into small florets

**2 egg yolks and 1 whole egg**

**2 tbsp water**

**salt & freshly ground black pepper to taste**

**¼ cup fresh parmesan cheese,** grated

**Cook** pasta according to the manufacturer's instructions.

**Heat** oil in a very large frypan or pot and fry bacon until it starts to crisp. Add garlic and cook about 30 seconds, without browning.

**Add** spinach to the pan and cook turning frequently until wilted (1-2 minutes). Remove from heat.

**Add** prepared broccoli to pasta pot in last 2 minutes of cooking.

**Lightly** beat egg yolks and whole egg with water and season with salt and pepper.

**Drain** pasta and broccoli then return to cooking pot, off the heat. Using a big spoon mix in egg and water mix and parmesan to fully coat pasta.

**Mix** through hot bacon and spinach, season with salt and lots of freshly ground pepper.

**Serve** at once accompanied with extra parmesan.

**Serves 2. Recipe easily doubles or trebles.**

**Make a menu match with:** *Fresh sliced oranges and pears drizzled with honey.*

## Soft Polenta with Mustard Chicken Sauce

*If you are looking for a dine and dash dinner that is big on satisfaction, it's hard to go past polenta or cornmeal. Quick to prepare, its creamy, almost fat-free smoothness goes well with a variety of sauces. See page 49 for more on polenta.*

**TO PREPARE:** 10 minutes   **TO COOK:** 15 minutes

**1 recipe cooked soft polenta** (see page 49)

**Chicken Sauce:**

**2 shallots or 1 small onion,** finely diced

**1 tsp butter**

**½ cup white wine**

**½ cup each cream and milk**

**2 tsp cornflour**

**1 tbsp Dijon mustard** or more to taste

**400g boneless chicken,** fat removed, cut in thin strips

**salt & freshly ground black pepper to taste**

**Garnish: ¼ cup parsley,** chopped or chives, chopped

**Make** the polenta. While it cooks prepare chicken sauce.

**Place** shallots or onions in a frypan with butter and wine and bring to a boil.

**Boil** until dry and just starting to brown.

**Add** cream and milk which has been mixed with cornflour and mustard. Add to pan.

**Stir** until boiling and lightly thickened.

**Mix** in chicken, reduce heat, cover and simmer gently 3-4 minutes or until cooked. Season with salt and freshly ground pepper to taste and mix in parsley or chives.

**To serve,** spoon a big dollop of polenta onto hot plates, spoon over sauce.

**Serves 4.**

**Make a menu match with:** *A crisp green salad.*

## Stephen Tindall's Lamb Shank Sauce for Pasta

*Over the winter, Cibo Restaurant served up this wonderful Lamb Shank Sauce on pasta. It would be nice on polenta too. If you prefer, the lamb shanks can be left whole and served with the sauce, like a casserole. The flavours improve on standing, so if you have time make it up a day ahead, chill and skim off any fat before reheating.*

**TO PREPARE:** 10-12 minutes    **TO COOK:** 2 hours 15 minutes

¼ cup soya or salad oil

6 lamb shanks

1 carrot, 1 large onion, 2-3 stalks celery all finely diced, 2 bay leaves, 3-4 sprigs thyme

1 tbsp flour

¼ cup tomato paste

1 cup red wine

6 cups beef stock

2 tbsp soya sauce

salt & freshly ground black pepper to taste

To serve: ¼ cup grated parmesan; 600-800g dried pasta, e.g. thick noodles; a little oil and grated lemon rind for pasta.

**Heat** oil in a very large heavy pot. Season shanks and brown in batches and put aside. Remove from pan. Drain off and discard most of oil.

**Add** vegetables and herbs and cook until lightly browned. Add flour and tomato paste and stir over heat 1 minute.

**Mix** red wine, stock and soya sauce into pan and bring to a simmer, stirring well to lift pan brownings.

**Add** lamb shanks back into sauce, cover and simmer gently for 2 hours, skimming off fat regularly.

**Lift** out shanks, remove meat from bone, (sauce can be strained of vegetables if preferred). Bring sauce to boil over high heat and boil hard 5-10 minutes stirring frequently until reduced to just coat the back of the spoon.

**Mix** in shank meat. Season to taste and bring to a simmer.

**Cook** 600-650g dried pasta, according to manufacturer's instructions. Drain and mix with a little oil and lemon rind and divide between 6 serving plates. Ladle sauce in the centre. Grate over parmesan.

**Serves 6-8.**

**Make a menu match with:** *A crisp green salad.*

## Bangers, Mash and Mushrooms

*Pakeha soul-food. This is great comfort fare, served up with a big pile of steaming baby bok choy and cooked pumpkin. The sauce is also great with steaks, or tossed through pasta.*

**TO PREPARE:** 10 minutes    **TO COOK:** 20 minutes

2-3 cups hot Roasted Garlic Mashed Potatoes (see page 71)

1 tbsp olive oil

1 clove garlic, crushed

250g fresh mushrooms, preferably flats

1½ cups chicken stock or 1 x 375ml carton

1 tbsp lemon juice, mixed with 2 tsp cornflour

salt & freshly ground black pepper to taste

2-4 good sausages, veal bratwurst are great

**Cook** potatoes for the mash, and while they cook, fry, bake or grill sausages and make mushroom sauce.

**To** make sauce: heat oil in a heavy frypan and add garlic, and mushrooms. Cook over high heat until the pan is dry and mushrooms start to brown, about 5 minutes.

**Add** stock and simmer 5 minutes. Mix lemon juice with cornflour. Stir into sauce until it lightly thickens.

**Season** with salt and freshly ground pepper to taste.

**Keep** warm and reheat when needed.

**Serve** a mound of hot mash with sausages. Pour over mushroom sauce. Serve lightly cooked greens on the side.

**Serves 2. Recipe easily doubles.**

**Make a menu match with:** *Fresh fruit salad.*

*Bangers, Mash and Mushrooms*

# A Solstice Dinner

*Country Style Cassoulet*

*Roasted Walnut, Orange and Beet Salad*

*Kiwifruit with Caramel, Grand Marnier and Spice Trail Biscotti*

## Country Style Cassoulet

*Traditional cassoulets tend to be incredibly rich and heavy. This easy version is wonderfully light and flavoursome. It makes a great winter feast. You need to start at least a day ahead to soak the beans. Like many bean-based dishes and casseroles, the flavour of this cassoulet improves the day after it is made. Most people won't have a single dish big enough to cook it in. I usually use two.*

**TO PREPARE:** 10 minutes    **TO COOK:** 3 hours 30 minutes

3½ **cups dried white beans** (use a mixture of lima and haricot)

¼ **cup olive oil**

8 **lamb shanks**

8 **chicken thighs**, bone in

4 **spicy sausages,** e.g. Julia Colbasse, diced

3 **large onions,** peeled and cut in wedges

1 **head garlic,** cloves peeled

3 **tbsp tomato paste**

2 x 400g **cans tomatoes in juice,** roughly chopped

2 **cups white wine**

6 **cups chicken stock**

8 **bay leaves**

4 **sprigs thyme**

**salt & freshly ground black pepper to taste**

**Pick** over beans and remove any stones.

**Soak** beans overnight in cold water, drain.

**Place** in a big pot with cold water to cover by 4cm and bring to a boil.

**Reduce** heat and simmer 30 minutes.

**Season** to taste and cook another 15 minutes.

**Drain** beans reserving 2 cups of their liquid. Preheat oven to 180°C.

**Heat** olive oil in a large frypan and brown off lamb shanks and chicken in batches, removing them as they are browned.

**Drain** off oil and discard.

**Divide** lamb shanks between 2 large casserole dishes or use one if all will fit into one. (Remember the beans and chicken are to come.)

**Reserve** chicken thighs to add to dish later. Add the sausage, onions and garlic to pan and cook gently until onions are clear. Add tomato paste, and stir over heat for 30 seconds.

**Add** tomatoes, wine, stock, herbs and reserved bean liquid. Bring to the boil. Season to taste, then pour over meat dividing evenly between 2 dishes.

**Cover** tightly and bake for 1¾ hours.

**Mix** beans and browned chicken pieces into the cassoulet, pressing to cover with sauce.

**Return** the baking dish to oven for 1 hour.

**Serve** each person a big scoop of beans and their juices topped with a lamb shank and a piece of chicken. Sprinkle topping over each serve. Cooked cassoulet freezes well.

**Serves 8.**

## Cassoulet Topping

2 **thick slices white bread**

**large handful parsley**

2 **cloves garlic,** peeled

2 **tsp fresh thyme leaves,** chopped

3 **tbsp olive oil**

**Purée** bread into fine crumbs.

**Blend** in all other ingredients until well combined.

**Spread** onto a baking tray and bake at 180°C for about 15 minutes until crisp, pale and golden.

**Store** in an airtight jar.

**Serves 8.**

**Make a menu match with:** *Salad of Bitter Greens and Grapefruit.*

## Sue Story's Lamb Tagine

*Sue Story teaches cooking classes in Auckland, and worked on this book as one of the recipe testers. This melt in your mouth lamb casserole is one of her specialties.*

**TO PREPARE:** 10 minutes    **TO COOK:** 1 hour 15 minutes

**1kg lean lamb,** cubed 3-4cm pieces

**2 tsp ground cumin**

**2 tsp ground coriander**

**1 tsp cinnamon**

**1 tsp ground ginger**

**1 tsp dried oregano**

**½ tsp cayenne,** to taste

**2 tbsp oil**

**1 large onion,** chopped

**1 cup dried apricots**

**1½ cups chicken stock** or 1 x 375ml carton

**salt & freshly ground black pepper to taste**

**Garnish: 1-2 tsp Harissa to taste.**

**Mix** all dry spices and herbs through the meat.

**Heat** half the oil in a large frypan over high heat.

**Add** half meat, spread out and brown on one side only.

**Remove** to a plate. Repeat, heating other half of oil to brown only one side of meat.

**Place** browned meat in a medium casserole dish or saucepan.

**Add** onion to the frypan to soften slightly, then add apricots and stock, stirring to incorporate all flavours and tasty bits in the pan.

**Tip** this into browned meat, stir and simmer gently for one hour. If using the oven, cook covered for 1 hour at 160°C or until the meat is tender.

**Season** to taste with salt, pepper and Harissa.

**Serves 5-6.**

**Make a menu match with:** *Plain couscous or Saffron Date and Almond Couscous.*

## Lemon Roast Chicken with Pumpkin and Onions

*An initial hot roast browns and crisps the skin and releases the fat of this tender moist chicken. The surrounding vegetables bulk out the meal and add rich flavour to the sauce.*

**TO PREPARE:** 10-15 minutes    **TO COOK:** 1 hour 15 minutes

**1 medium-sized fresh chicken,** visible fat removed

**olive oil and salt,** to rub

**400g-600g pumpkin,** peeled and cut into 4cm wedges

**2 cloves garlic,** sliced

**4-6 small-medium onions,** unpeeled, washed, cut in half

**finely grated rind and juice of ½ lemon,** no pith

**1½ cups chicken stock** or 1 x 375ml carton

**1 tsp fresh rosemary,** chopped

**salt & freshly ground black pepper to taste**

**Preheat** oven to 220°C.

**Rub** chicken all over with olive oil, sprinkle with salt and set on a rack in a deepish roasting dish. Roast at 220°C for 20 minutes until browned.

**Take** out of oven, remove fat from dish and place bird in bottom of dish.

**Reduce** oven temperature to 200°C. Arrange pumpkin, garlic, and onions cut-side down around chicken. (Leaving skins on protects onions and they can be popped out of their skins to eat.) Mix lemon rind and juice with ½ cup of stock and pour over chicken. Sprinkle over rosemary.

**Bake** at 180°C for 45-55 minutes, until juices run clear, basting chicken 2-3 times with pan juices during cooking. Lift chicken out of pan onto a serving platter with vegetables. Place pan on heat, add remaining stock, adjust seasonings to taste and simmer. If desired, thicken sauce with 2 tsp cornflour mixed with a dash of water.

**Serves 4.**

**M**ash. *Creamy smooth and soothing, mash is our favourite comfort fare. It's hardly surprising that we like it so much. After all vegetable mashed in various forms is what we all grew up on.*

*Since those early days mash has come to mean a lot more than potatoes. You can make it with any kind of root vegetable, as well as pumpkin, beans, lentils, in fact anything you can physically mash. Mash takes well to flavourings – garlic, wilted rocket, chillies, lemon rind, herbs and ginger are some successful integrations.*

*More rustic than a purée, mash is usually made by mashing cooked foods, rather than puréeing them. Mash needs to be seasoned well – it absorbs a lot of salt and pepper. Mash is one of the best partners for gravy – slow cooked casseroles and tagines, pan cooked steak with a sauce, or roast meat and gravy. You'll be amazed at how much mash people will eat! For mashed potatoes I usually allow 1 large potato per serve, plus 2 extra for good measure – i.e. for 4 people, 6 potatoes.*

## Olive Oil Mashed Potatoes – Master Recipe

*You need a good, starchy, boiling potato here, nothing waxy. Suitable varieties include White Delight, Rua, Jersey Bennes, Nadine, Fresia, Ilam Hardy, Iwa and Sebago.*

**Place** 6 large mashing potatoes, peeled, cut in half or quarters if large, in a pot with cold water to cover. **Season** with a good teaspoon of salt. **Bring** to a boil and simmer until tender. **Drain** then return to heat and cook at lowest temperature for 2-3 minutes to dry off potatoes. **Push** through a sieve or mash until fine. (Don't ever blend in a food processor – you'll end up with glue.) **Heat** 1/4 cup of extra virgin olive oil and 2 tbsp butter in a pan or microwave bowl until butter is melted. **Add** to potatoes, season with salt and pepper and 1-2 tbsp lemon juice or white wine vinegar to taste. Mash until light and fluffy. **Serves 4-6.**

## Roasted Garlic Mashed Potatoes

**Use** 1 head roasted garlic cooked in oil. **Heat** to warm through and use in place of oil and butter mix in master recipe (see above). **Season** to taste.

## Kumara Mash

**Use** peeled chopped kumara in place of potatoes in master recipe (see above), or a 50-50 kumara and potato mix. **Use** an olive oil and butter mix to mash, or just plain butter. **Season** to taste.

## Parrot Mash

**Use** 50-50 carrots and parsnips in master recipe (see left). They will take longer than potatoes to cook. **Mash** with butter. **Season** to taste.

## Parsnip and Rocket Mash

**Use** 6 large parsnips in master recipe (see left). **Add** a bunch of chopped rocket or watercress to the pot about 5 minutes before parsnips are cooked. **Mash** or purée in a blender with butter or olive oil. **Season** to taste.

## White Bean Mash

*This lovely rustic purée makes a good partner to pan cooked steaks and mushroom sauce, as well as hearty meat casseroles. If you prefer a chunkier texture, purée onions and garlic then mash in beans and flavourings.*

**You** need 3 cups cooked white beans to start – if using canned, drain and rinse. **Preheat** oven to 160°C. **Peel** and roughly chop 1 large red onion and 8 cloves garlic, place in a roasting dish with 1 tsp fresh rosemary leaves and pour over 1/4 cup oil. **Bake** for about 40 minutes until tender and lightly golden. **Add** cooked beans to dish and cook a further 10 minutes. **Purée** onions, garlic and beans and the finely grated rind of 1/2 lemon (no pith) in a blender until smooth, adding a little oil or water if required to get a creamy consistency. **Season** to taste with salt and pepper. Serve hot. Beans reheat well in a pot or microwave. **Makes about 3 cups, for 4-6 serves.**

# Naan Bread

*This soft puffy bread makes a great mop for winter soups and stews.*

**TO PREPARE:** 15 minutes + 30-40 minutes rising  **TO COOK:** 4-5 minutes

**6 cups high grade flour,** plus extra flour for kneading

**2 tsp salt**

**1 cup hot water**

**1 tbsp sugar**

**1 cup unsweetened yoghurt**

**1 tbsp dried yeast**

**2 eggs**

**6 tbsp butter,** melted

**Combine** flour and salt in a large mixing bowl.

**Mix** hot water, sugar and yoghurt in another bowl – mix should be lukewarm.

**Stir** in yeast and leave for 5 minutes.

**Beat** eggs and melted butter into yeast mixture.

**Combine** with flour, stirring until mixture has combined.

**Turn** out onto a lightly floured board and continue kneading until mix has come together into a smooth soft dough (10 minutes). Extra flour may be required for kneading.

**Place** aside in warm place, covered until doubled in bulk (30-40 minutes).

**Lightly** flour a board and turn out the dough.

**Knead** for 2-3 minutes until smooth, silky and elastic.

**Take** golf ball-sized pieces of dough and work into balls.

**Roll** or press balls on a lightly floured surface, flattening to 1cm thickness. Give them a light pull to stretch dough a little.

**Place** 3 or 4 breads (as will fit) on a lightly floured oven tray or baking stone and grill under high heat until golden brown and puffy on one side, (1-2 minutes).

**Turn** over and cook the other side.

**Repeat** until all breads are cooked. Reheat in tinfoil if required. Serve plain or brush with butter or oil (plain or flavoured).

**Makes about 15 large naans.**

## 'Carta de Musica' — Sardinian Sheet Music Bread

*This crisp flatbread makes an excellent accompaniment to salads, pâtés and dips.*

**TO PREPARE:** 20 minutes + rising     **TO COOK:** 8-10 minutes

**2 cups high grade flour**

**3/4 cup fine semolina**

**1 tsp salt**

**1 cup water,** approximately

**sea salt**

**Combine** dry ingredients. Slowly add water mixing to a soft but not sticky dough. Rest for 10 minutes.

**Preheat** oven to 220-250°C.

**Divide** dough into 12 separate balls.

**Roll** each ball out until paper thin on a lightly oiled surface, preferably in the shape of a narrow sheet of paper.

**Brush** dough with rosemary and garlic-infused olive oil (see below) or plain olive oil if preferred.

**Sprinkle** with sea salt. If desired top with a light grating of parmesan cheese or chopped herbs.

**Cook** 8-10 minutes on a hot pizza stone or baking tray or until crisp and golden. Store in an airtight container.

**Makes 12 flatbreads.**

## Rosemary and Garlic-Infused Olive Oil

*Oils can be infused with a variety of flavourings — coffee, lemon or orange rinds, and chillies all work with great success. Follow the method below.*

**Gently** heat 1/2 cup extra virgin olive oil; 2 tbsp fresh chopped rosemary; 1 peeled and crushed clove garlic; 1 fresh bay leaf; 1 chilli. Do not overheat. **Cool**. Store in a clean, sealed bottle in a cool place. Oil will keep for a couple of months. **Makes 1/2 cup.**

*Sue Story's Lamb Tagine with Naan Bread (top), Carta de Musica (side)*

*Salmon and Lemon*

*Risotto, page 87*

# $\mathcal{S}$pring

**And so it begins again.**

**The first new growth,**

**a marvel of nature when sap runs,**

buds burst and seeds sprout. Tastes lighten, seeking spring's pure freshness – the first asparagus, the sweetness of early first strawberries, new spring greens, sweet tiny artichokes – nothing more needed than a splash of burnt butter, some good olive oil or the best balsamic vinegar. Cos lettuce makes a return to our spring plates in our favourite Caesar salad. Citrus takes the stage as spring's star tart flavouring. Enhancing our sense of freshness, it turns up in lemony salmon risottos, orange and sesame stir-fries, tangy noodle broths and stylish couscous plates. We take the chill off spring evenings with exciting soups in French and Vietnamese styles, spike our stir-fries with chillies and spring herbs, and eat them wrapped up in crisp lettuce leaves.

As the weather settles, we look for the freshest of seafoods – and serve them up marinated in salads, simmered with exotic Brazilian flavours and gently cooked in flavoursome broths.

And then there are the freshest, crisp, sweet oysters to be eaten before summer, when they will turn spongy and spawn. It's a time of renewal, a time to rethink the way we cook and eat, to be adventurous with our food, to seek out new tastes and good company to share them with.

*O*yster pleasures. There is little doubt that the world's best oysters are found in areas where water temperatures are chilly. Crispness is an unusual way to describe an oyster's texture, but cold water oysters like the Bluff have just that – a real bite. If you try an oyster over the summer months you will encounter the opposite – while oysters are spawning they have a spongy, milky coarse-grained texture that comes from being ovaparious (milk-producing). And that applies to the males too, as they switch sex and become female during spawning. While it won't make you sick, it's a good enough reason not to eat them over the summer months. Make the most of their immaculate freshness and sensational taste during winter and early spring.

Immaculate freshness is the key to oysters of any description – a rotten oyster can kill you. As all our oysters come ready shucked, you need to be very astute in your purchasing. Look for oysters with a clear greyish-white colour and a glossy appearance. They should smell of the sea, and not anything else. Avoid them if they are yellowish or slimy looking.

Oysters freeze exceptionally well with little or no loss of texture or flavour. Keep a supply on hand for spur of the moment eating. Thaw them just before serving, dropping into salted cold water to help them plump up.

## Oysters on the rocks with a dash of:

**Sake** with thin sliced pickled ginger • **Lime** juice and black pepper • **Sherry** • **Fish sauce**, sweet Thai chilli sauce and lime juice in equal parts • **50-50** light soya sauce and sake • **Balsamic** vinegar.

## Thai Oyster Salad on the Half Shell

**Mix** together 3 tbsp lemon juice, 1 tbsp Thai fish sauce, 1 tbsp brown sugar or palm sugar, 1 tsp tamarind paste, 1 tsp chilli paste, finely grated rind of 1 lemon, 4 crushed cloves garlic, 2 spring onions very finely chopped, 1/4 cup fresh chopped mint leaves. **Remove** 2 dozen oysters from their shells and combine gently with flavour mix. **Clean** shells, then return dressed oysters to shells. **Chill** for up to 1 hour before serving. **Garnish** with extra mint leaves. **Makes enough for 2 dozen oysters.**

## Gratinéed Half Shell Oysters with Lemon Herb Crumb

**Sort** over 2 dozen oysters on half shell, removing any broken shells. **Combine** 1 cup fresh breadcrumbs, finely grated rind of 1 lemon, 1 clove garlic, crushed, pinch cayenne pepper, 1 tbsp pesto and 2 tbsp melted butter. **Spread** on a baking tray and bake at 180°C for 15-20 minutes until crisp and pale gold. **Brush** a little lemon juice over each oyster, top with crumb and place in a 250°C oven for 3-4 minutes – just to warm through. **Makes enough for 2 dozen oysters.**

## Pico de Gallo with Oysters

*This versatile Mexican sauce is standard table fare on tables near the Mexican border. It makes a great accompaniment to corn chips and fresh vegetable bites and is excellent as a topping for fresh oysters on the half shell.*

**Combine** 2 tomatoes diced into 1cm cubes, with 1 small finely diced onion, 4 minced cloves garlic, 2 minced chillies, 4 tbsp chopped coriander, 2 tbsp lime juice, 2 tbsp olive oil and salt and a pinch of sugar to taste. Let combined ingredients stand for 30 minutes. Sauce can be made up to 8 hours ahead of time and chilled. **Makes enough for 2 dozen oysters.**

## Smoked Salmon and Leek Chowder

*Any kind of smoked fish can be used to make this tasty chowder, but smoked salmon gives the most elegant result. Chowders by definition are thick and chunky and generally benefit from being made a day ahead of time to allow flavours to mingle and develop. Refrigerate and reheat to serve.*

**TO PREPARE:** 10 minutes    **TO COOK:** 30 minutes

**2 tbsp butter**

**2 spring onions,** finely chopped

**3 large leeks,** cleaned and finely diced

**6 cups fish stock or salmon stock** (see page 106)

**3 medium potatoes,** peeled and diced into 2cm cubes

**1 cup cream**

**200g-250g smoked salmon, offcuts are fine,**

finely diced

**1 tbsp chervil or dill,** chopped

**several shakes tabasco**

**salt & freshly ground black pepper to taste**

**Heat** butter in a large heavy pot and gently cook spring onions and leeks for 4-5 minutes until softened.

**Add** fish stock and potato.

**Bring** to boil then reduce heat and simmer 25 minutes or until potato is tender.

**Stir** in cream, smoked salmon, chervil or dill, tabasco and salt and pepper. Bring back to a simmer.

**Serve** hot. Soup flavour develops further on standing.

**Serves 6.**

**Make a menu match with:** *Herb Crusted Lamb Racks, Roasted Garlic Mashed Potatoes and Sautéed Spinach.*

## Vietnamese Chicken Noodle Soup

*This clear refreshing soup is deceptively filling. The broth makes a great base for all manner of additions – here I have used chicken, vegetables and noodles, but a seafood soup could be made using the same flavourings and seafood.*

**TO PREPARE:** 10 minutes    **TO COOK:** 20 minutes

**Broth:**

**8 cups chicken stock**

**6 x 1cm slices fresh ginger root**

**4 whole star anise**

**¼ cup fish sauce**

**2 tbsp lime juice**

**1 tbsp sugar**

**Accompaniments:**

**250g rice stick noodles,** soaked in hot water 5-8 minutes

**250g raw chicken,** very thinly sliced

**3 spring onions,** thinly sliced

**1 packet (250g) bean sprouts**

**2 red chillies,** thinly sliced, **or a spoonful of chilli paste**

**¼ cup coriander and/or mint,** chopped

**2 limes,** cut in wedges

**Heat** chicken stock with ginger, star anise, fish sauce, lime juice and sugar.

**Simmer** 15 minutes then strain out solids. Soak rice sticks in hot water 5-8 minutes. Drain.

**Add** chicken and bring to a simmer for 1 minute, then immediately add drained rice sticks and all other ingredients, except lime wedges.

**Bring** back to a simmer and serve at once. Garnish with lime wedges.

**Serves 6.**

**Make a menu match with:** *Beijing Duck Salad Pancakes.*

## Vietnamese Fisherman's Soup

*This stunning soup is really a meal in itself. The recipe is one which appears in various forms in Vietnamese cookbooks. Many recipes just use water as a base. I prefer the extra flavour you get from cooking up the prawn shells first. Suit yourself.*

**TO PREPARE:** 10 minutes    **TO COOK:** 30 minutes

**1kg whole green prawns,** raw

**¼ cup oil**

**6 cups water**

**400g-500g boneless fresh fish,** cut into 2-3cm pieces

**¼ cup fish sauce**

**1 onion,** thinly sliced

**3 cloves garlic,** crushed

**3 stems lemon grass,** white end only, peeled and crushed, or **finely grated rind of 1 lemon or lime**

**1-2 tsp sugar to taste**

**¼ fresh pineapple,** flesh cut in bite-sized chunks

**2-3 tbsp tamarind paste** mixed with ¼ cup boiling water

**salt to taste**

**2 tomatoes,** peeled, core removed and diced

**2 chillies,** minced

**Garnish: 1 packet mung bean sprouts; 1 bunch of spinach,** washed and finely chopped; **3 spring onions; 2 tbsp each fresh coriander and mint;** chopped.

**Remove** head and shells from prawns and place in a pot with half the oil. Fry until pink then use a masher to crush and release flavours. If just using water omit this step.

**Add** water and simmer for 20 minutes, strain and reserve liquids to one side.

**Mix** prawn meat and fish with half of the fish sauce.

**Set** aside in fridge while all other ingredients are prepared.

**Heat** rest of oil in a big pot and gently fry onion and garlic until clear.

**Add** lemon grass or rind, sugar and pineapple and stir-fry for 1 minute.

**Pour** over hot prawn stock or water, mix in tamarind paste, rest of fish sauce and salt to taste.

**Bring** to a boil and simmer 2-3 minutes. Soup can be prepared ahead of time to this point. Just before serving bring to boil.

**Add** tomatoes, chillies, bean sprouts, spinach, spring onions, coriander and mint.

**Bring** to a boil, then add seafood, stir over heat to evenly combine, let it just come to the boil and then serve at once.

**Serves 6 large or 8 smallish serves.**

## Cheat's Consommé with Coriander and Wontons

*This is the ultimate cheat's soup – it looks and tastes like hours of effort has gone into it while in fact it takes just a few minutes to throw together. Buy frozen wontons in Asian supermarkets or the freezer cabinet of large supermarkets.*

**TO PREPARE:** 5 minutes    **TO COOK:** 8-10 minutes

**4 cups chicken stock**

**pinch of sugar**

**1 tbsp fish sauce**

**16 prepared wontons or ravioli**

**Optional: baby bok choy, carrots, or leeks,** sliced

**1 fresh chilli,** finely diced

**1 bunch coriander,** finely chopped, coarse stems removed

**1 spring onion,** finely sliced

**salt & freshly ground black pepper to taste**

**1 tbsp lime or lemon juice**

**Heat** stock, sugar and fish sauce. Bring to a simmer and add wontons or ravioli. Cook gently until just tender.

**Add** any optional vegetables in last 4 minutes of cooking.

**Add** chilli, coriander and spring onion. Season with salt and freshly ground black pepper and lime or lemon juice.

**Serves 4 small bowls or 2 large meals.**

**Make a menu match with:** *Teppenyaki Beef.*

*A Weekend Dinner with Friends*

Bouillabaisse with Rouille and Croûtons

Caesar Salad

Brie and fresh fruits

# Bouillabaisse

*Whenever I get lucky with my fishing line I make this divine soup. The heads and bones go in to make the stock and the fillets get lightly poached in the soup just prior to serving. I was first introduced to Bouillabaisse by master cuisinère, friend and one-time cook to President Mitterand, Daniele Delpeuch. Any kind of seafood can be added to the base broth – it tastes better if you can use 2-3 different kinds of fish. Prawns just make it look special, but the soup does not need them for flavour. In France, the fish is usually served first on a plate, with the broth to follow, topped with garlicky, hot rouille croûtons. Aïoli can be used instead of rouille. The French use more oil and boil their fish hard for about 10 minutes. I prefer mine with less oil and just cooked fish.*

**TO PREPARE:** 20 minutes   **TO COOK:** 45 minutes

**½ cup olive oil**

**2 medium onions,** finely chopped

**1 large leek,** finely chopped

**1 stalk celery,** finely chopped

**3-4 bay leaves**

**4 large garlic cloves,** chopped

**2 tbsp tomato paste**

**1-2 tsp chilli paste,** to taste

**2 cups dry white wine**

**big pinch saffron threads**

**1 tsp honey**

**2 x 400g cans tomatoes in juice,** chopped **or 1kg**

**fresh tomatoes,** peeled and chopped

**12 cups fish stock** (see page 106)

**salt & freshly ground black pepper to taste**

**about 1kg various firm fish,** boneless, e.g. monkfish, john dory, hapuka or snapper, cut in 3-4 pieces

**500-700g fresh mussels,** scrubbed

**Optional: 8-16 large raw prawns,** cleaned

**To Garnish: Rouille Croûtons**

**Heat** oil in a large pot and gently cook onions for 10-15 minutes until clear.

**Add** leek and celery and cook a further 10 minutes.

**Add** bay leaves, garlic, tomato paste and chilli paste. Sizzle a few seconds.

**Mix** in wine, saffron, honey and tomatoes.

**Cook** for 20 minutes over low heat.

**Add** fish stock and season to taste. Bring back to a simmer.

**Just** before serving, add mussels and cook until they open (or steam separately then add back into the soup with their juices). Discard any mussels that don't open.

**Add** fish fillets and cook gently for 2-3 minutes until just cooked. Divide between hot soup bowls.

**Serve** each bowl topped with a croûton (see below), spread with rouille (see below), and pass around extra rouille and croûtons separately.

**Makes 8 large servings.**

## Rouille

**1 large potato,** boiled and puréed, or mashed

**6 cloves garlic,** peeled and minced

**1-2 tsp chilli paste,** to taste

**1 egg yolk**

**salt to taste**

**½ cup extra virgin olive oil**

**Purée** or mash all ingredients together, adding salt to taste. Stored in the fridge, rouille will keep for 2-3 days.

## Croûtons

**Cut** 2cm slices of French or rustic country bread on an angle.

**Place** on a baking tray and bake at 180°C for about 15 minutes until crisp.

**Store** in an airtight container and re-crisp in oven for 5 minutes if required.

## Marinated Salmon Salad

*A quick sear and then into a marinade of vermouth, orange juice, and lime juice renders the salmon in this great little salad succulent and juicy. This method of pickling cooked fish, known as "escabese" (escabeche to the Spanish), was used in earlier times as a way of making fish last. It's also a great recipe for fresh trout.*

**TO PREPARE:** 15 minutes + marinating **TO COOK:** 10 minutes

**500g-700g fresh salmon,** in the piece, skin and bones removed

**salt & freshly ground black pepper to taste**

**1/3 cup extra virgin olive oil**

**1/2 cup each dry vermouth and fresh orange juice**

**1/4 cup lime or lemon juice**

**1 tbsp white wine vinegar**

**finely grated rind of 1 lemon and 1 orange,** no pith

**To serve: several handfuls of fresh watercress; 3 oranges,** peeled and segmented; **3-4 tbsp each of fresh coriander and mint,** chopped.

**Optional: 2 bunches asparagus,** ends snapped off and discarded, spears boiled for 1 minute, then cooled.

**Cut** salmon into slices about 2cm thick. Season with salt and freshly ground black pepper.

**Heat** oil in a frypan and once hot, quickly fry pieces for about 20-30 seconds on each side.

**Remove** at once from pan to prevent further cooking – flesh should only be just cooked on the outside. Place in a shallow dish. Mix together vermouth, orange, lemon or lime juices, vinegar and rinds and pour over fish.

**Cover** and refrigerate for 12-48 hours.

**Just** before serving, check seasoning and adjust to taste. Mix through watercress, toss through oranges, herbs and optional asparagus.

**Serves 6 as a main and 8-10 as a first course.**

## Grilled Chicken Caesar Salad

*This is the best dressing for Caesar I have come across. Leave the chicken out for a classic Caesar.*

**TO PREPARE:** 10-15 minutes    **TO COOK:** 10 minutes

**4 chicken thighs,** skin removed

**finely grated rind of 1/2 lemon**

**salt & freshly ground black pepper to taste**

**about 1 tbsp oil**

**Optional: 4 eggs,** preferably free range, 1 tbsp each salt and vinegar

**1 large head romaine** or other crisp lettuce, leaves washed and dried

**1 x quantity Caesar dressing,** see below

**12 Croûtons** (see page 81)

**1/4 cup parmesan cheese,** shaved with a potato peeler

**freshly ground black pepper to taste**

**Mix** chicken with lemon rind, salt and pepper.

**Heat** a frypan with a little oil. Pan-fry chicken about 6 -8 minutes until cooked through. Remove and stand while preparing salad.

**Break** optional eggs into a pot of simmering water to which 1 tbsp each of salt and vinegar has been added.

**Simmer** gently for about 1 minute until egg whites are set, remove with a slotted spoon and put to one side.

**Place** lettuce leaves in a large salad bowl.

**Toss** dressing through lettuce. Slice chicken pieces and add. Throw on croûtons, sprinkle with parmesan and grind over black pepper. Toss it all together. Divide between 4 serving plates and if desired, top each with the poached egg.

**To make Caesar Dressing:** Heat a frypan with 1 tbsp oil. **Add** 5-6 anchovies and 2 cloves crushed garlic. **Gently** fry, stirring until anchovies soften and break up. Remove from heat and mix in 1/2 cup cream and 2 tbsp lemon juice. **Store** in fridge; dressing will keep 2-3 days.

**Serves 4.**

*Marinated Salmon Salad*

## Chinese Hot and Spicy Pork Salad Cups

*The printer I work with in Hong Kong is a self-confessed foodie who always knows the best place to eat anything. He introduced me to this combination of stir-fried pork with crispy noodles rolled up in crunchy lettuce leaves which is a popular Hong Kong menu item. I have used radicchio in place of regular crisp green lettuce.*

**TO PREPARE:** 5 minutes    **TO COOK:** 8 minutes

**200-250g pork mince or chicken mince**

**1 tbsp sweet Thai chilli sauce**

**1 tbsp sesame oil**

**1 tbsp fresh root ginger,** minced

**¼ cup oyster sauce**

**1 x 320g can water chestnuts,** rinsed and thinly sliced

**2 spring onions,** sliced thinly

**¼ cup peanuts or cashews,** roasted

**1 carrot,** peeled, shredded or grated

**2 tbsp coriander or mint,** chopped

**2 large handfuls crispy noodles**

**2 heads of radicchio lettuce or 1 large green crunchy lettuce,** leaves carefully separated and washed

**Combine** mince with chilli sauce, oil and root ginger.
**Stand** 5 minutes or up to 8 hours in fridge.
**Heat** a wok or large frypan and fry pork over high heat until browned and cooked through, about 5-8 minutes.
**Mix** in oyster sauce and remove from heat.
**Mix** water chestnuts, spring onions, peanuts or cashews, carrot, coriander or mint, and crispy noodles through meat.
**Use** 3-4 lettuce leaves to make a basket in each bowl. Spoon mixture into lettuce cups.
**Serve** at once. Eat by rolling up the stir-fry mix in lettuce leaves.

**Serves 2.**

## Beef Teppenyaki

*This is an easy stir-fry with a Japanese twist. Take care not to overcook the beef – once added the dish should only be cooked for about 3 minutes.*

**TO PREPARE:** 5 minutes + 10 minutes standing beef    **TO COOK:** 5 minutes

**2 tbsp soya sauce**

**1-2 tsp hot chilli sauce,** to taste

**1 tbsp sesame oil**

**2 tbsp root ginger,** grated

**¼ cup sake or sweet sherry or mirin**

**1 tbsp rice wine vinegar or wine vinegar**

**1 tbsp sugar**

**200-250g lean beef steak,** e.g. rump, sliced in thin strips

**1 tbsp oil**

**2 spring onions,** peeled and thinly sliced

**200g mushrooms,** thinly sliced

**1 red pepper or roasted red pepper,** cut in thin matchstick strips

**Optional: ¼ cup pickled ginger,** finely sliced as garnish

**Combine** soya sauce, hot chilli sauce, sesame oil, ginger, sherry or mirin, vinegar and sugar in a clean bowl or plastic bag.
**Mix** thinly sliced meat through marinade meat into thin strips and mix through marinade. Leave for 10-15 minutes.
**Heat** oil in a large wok or frypan and cook onions, mushrooms and pepper for 2 minutes stirring frequently.
**Lift** meat from marinade and drain, reserving marinade.
**Add** to pan and cook over very high heat for 2-3 minutes until cooked. Add reserved marinade back to pan and heat through.
**Serve** over rice, at once garnished with optional pickled ginger. Accompany with rice.

**Serves 2.**

**Make a menu match with:** *Perfect Rice and lightly cooked baby bok choy.*

## One Pan Chicken Stir-fry with Chilli Peanut Sauce

*Great for busy weeknights, this flavour packed stir-fry can be made with any type of thinly sliced protein and vegetables – beef, pork, tofu or fish. If using light vegetables such as bean sprouts, snow peas etc., add just before serving.*

**TO PREPARE:** 8 minutes   **TO COOK:** 5-6 minutes

**400g-500g fresh dense mixed vegetables,** e.g. broccoli, carrots, zucchini, peppers, chopped

**2 tbsp oil**

**1 tsp each crushed garlic and minced root ginger**

**2 tbsp soya sauce**

**1 tbsp fish sauce**

**½ cup water**

**2-3 tbsp sweet Thai chilli sauce,** to taste

**250g boneless chicken,** thinly sliced

**1 heaped tbsp peanut butter**

**2 tbsp coriander or mint,** chopped

**To serve: 2 cups cooked rice or noodles**

**Place** vegetables in a microwave bowl with 2 tablespoons water. Cover and cook for 3 minutes. Alternatively, steam until nearly tender.

**Heat** oil in a large wok or pan.

**Add** garlic and ginger and sizzle for a few seconds.

**Add** soya sauce, fish sauce, water and sweet Thai chilli sauce to taste. Bring to a simmer.

**Mix** in chicken, cover and simmer gently for 3-4 minutes until cooked. Add peanut butter, stirring until dissolved.

**Mix** in cooked vegetables and fresh coriander or mint and bring back to a simmer. Serve immediately.

**Serve** over rice or noodles.

**Serves 2. Recipe doubles easily.**

**Make a menu match with:** *Cheat's Consommé with Coriander and Wontons and Fruit Crumble with Ginger, Cardamom and Cashews.*

## Orange and Sesame Cervena Stir-fry

*Beef can be used instead of Cervena for this easy combination. As with all stir-fries, have all the ingredients prepared ready to cook before you start.*

**TO PREPARE:** 10 minutes   **TO COOK:** 6-8 minutes

**2 bunches asparagus,** ends snapped and discarded or

**1 head broccoli,** cut into small pieces

**2 carrots,** cut in small batons

**200g mushrooms,** thinly sliced

**1 tsp fresh ginger,** minced

**2 cloves garlic,** crushed

**finely grated rind of ½ orange**

**400g Cervena (or beef),** thinly sliced, with no fat or sinew

**1 tbsp oil,** e.g. sunflower or soya

**2 tsp sesame oil**

**2 tbsp oyster sauce**

**juice of 1 orange**

**dash chilli sauce**

**Garnish: 2-3 tbsp sesame seeds,** toasted; **1 spring onion,** chopped; **and/or 2-3 tbsp fresh coriander,** chopped

**Boil,** steam or microwave vegetables until almost tender.

**Cool** under cold water, drain and reserve.

**Mix** ginger, garlic and orange rind through sliced meat.

**Heat** both oils in a wok or heavy pan, add half meat and stir-fry 2-3 minutes over high heat until just browned – do not overcook. Remove, reheat pan and cook other half.

**Mix** in cooked vegetables, oyster sauce, orange juice and chilli sauce, and using a big spoon, toss over heat until heated through. Return cooked meat to pan to heat through.

**Pile** onto a heated serving plate and sprinkle over sesame seeds and spring onion and/or coriander. Serve at once.

**Serves 4.**

**Make a menu match with:** *Perfect Rice and Naan Bread.*

# Huntsman's Pasta

*Great for a quick whip-up dinner, this easy pasta can be made with any type of full flavoured cured sausage.*

**TO PREPARE:** 5 minutes    **TO COOK:** 10 minutes

**500g dried pasta shapes,** e.g. tubes

**2 tsp fennel seeds**

**2 tbsp olive oil**

**2 rashers bacon,** diced

**150g Huntsman's sausage or other garlic sausage,** diced

**2 cloves garlic,** peeled and crushed

**1 tsp fresh rosemary,** chopped

**1 red or roasted pepper,** cored, seeded and diced

**2 x 400g cans tomatoes in juice,** chopped

**4 zucchini,** cut in matchsticks

**¼ cup cream**

**salt & freshly ground black pepper to taste**

**Garnish: parmesan cheese,** grated

**Cook** pasta according to manufacturer's instructions.

**Heat** a large frypan and toast fennel seeds until they start to "pop". Remove and roughly crush.

**Add** oil to frypan and fry bacon and sausage until fat starts to run.

**Mix** in crushed fennel seeds, garlic and rosemary and cook a few seconds more.

**Mix** in red pepper, tomatoes, zucchini and cream, bring to a simmer and cook gently for 5 minutes until zucchini is almost tender.

**Drain** cooked pasta, return to its cooking pot and pour over sauce. Mix sauce through pasta over heat for 1 minute to combine flavours. Adjust seasonings to taste.

**Serve** accompanied with fresh parmesan.

**Serves 4.**

**Make a menu match with:** *Crusty bread.*

# Salmon and Lemon Risotto

*Mixing the salmon with lemon rind and pepper before cooking gives it a lot more flavour when it is cooked. Use any kind of fresh fish and leeks, asparagus or beans.*

**TO PREPARE:** 5 minutes    **TO COOK:** 25 minutes

**finely grated rind of 1 lemon,** no pith

**salt & freshly ground black pepper to taste**

**300g-400g boneless fresh salmon,** cut into 2cm cubes

**2 tbsp olive oil**

**1 onion,** finely diced

**1 leek,** halved, washed and sliced in thin rounds, including green ends

**2 cups Italian short grain rice,** e.g. Carnaroli or Arborio

**½ cup white wine**

**4 cups fish or chicken stock,** hot

**big pinch saffron threads**

**2 tbsp lemon juice**

**lemon wedges to serve**

**Mix** lemon rind and pepper through diced fish.

**Heat** oil in a medium-large, heavy based pot and cook onion and leek over gentle heat until onion is clear.

**Add** rice and stir over heat another 1 minute. Add wine and stir until evaporated.

**Add** hot stock, saffron and salt to taste. Once mix boils reduce heat to low simmer. Simmer for exactly 18 minutes, stirring now and then. Rice should be sloppy.

**Mix** in fish and lemon juice and adjust seasonings. Press fish into rice to cover.

**Cover** pot and cook a further 2 minutes without stirring. Remove from heat and stand, without uncovering for 1-2 minutes before serving. If risotto looks dry, add a dash more stock.

**Serves 4.**

**Variation:** include chopped beans or asparagus and add in last 5 minutes of cooking.

## Carnival Couscous with Chicken

*Once you get into using couscous you'll find it as useful a staple as rice or pasta. Add chick peas, artichokes and peppers to make a good stand alone vegetarian dish or serve as an accompaniment to barbecues and grills.*

**TO PREPARE:** 10 minutes   **TO COOK:** 25 minutes

**2 chicken breasts,** beaten out flat to 1.5cm thickness

**Marinade: 2 tbsp lemon juice; 1 tsp cumin powder; 1 tsp Harissa or chilli paste** to taste; **salt & freshly ground black pepper.**

**1½ cups boiling water**

**¾ cup instant couscous or bulgur wheat**

**juice and finely grated rind of ½ lemon,** no pith

**½ cup fresh coriander, or mint or parsley,** chopped

**1 spring onion,** finely chopped

**¼ cup toasted pinenuts**

**Optional additions: 1 can chick peas,** rinsed and drained; **1 can artichokes,** drained and sliced; **flesh of 1 roasted red pepper,** cut 2cm pieces.

**salt & freshly ground black pepper to taste**

**Flatten** chicken breasts with a rolling pin between sheets of plastic wrap to 1.5cm thickness. Season with salt and pepper. Mix in lemon juice, cumin, and harissa or chilli paste. Leave chicken to marinate for 10-20 minutes.

**Pour** boiling water over couscous in a large bowl and leave to absorb (10 minutes). Mix in lemon juice and rind, coriander or mint, spring onion, pinenuts and other optional ingredients and season liberally with salt and pepper to taste.

**Heat** a little oil in a heavy pan and cook chicken for 4-5 minutes on each side, until cooked through. While chicken cooks, microwave or steam couscous to heat through.

**Remove** chicken from pan and rest 2-3 minutes before slicing. Pile hot couscous onto 2 serving plates. Slice chicken and fan slices over the top.

**Serves 2.**

## Beijing Duck Salad Pancakes

*Into the middle of the table – a stack of fresh chewy Chinese pancakes and 4 bowls – shredded cooked duck or chicken, hoisin sauce, spring onions and crispy lettuce. It's a simple formula which makes for thoroughly convivial dining. If you can't be bothered with making the pancakes, you can adapt the concept using soft flatbreads, like mountain bread – brush with a little sesame oil to get a better flavour comparison.*

**TO PREPARE:** 5 minutes

**2 cups shredded cooked duck meat or chicken,** no fat or bones, crisp skin optional

**½ cup hoisin sauce**

**3 spring onions,** halved lengthwise, cut into 4cm lengths

**½ crisp iceberg lettuce,** finely shredded

**1 recipe Chinese Grilled Pancakes** (see page 95), **or**

**4 slices flatbread,** cooked, brushed sparsely with **sesame oil** and cut into small rectangles

**Place** everything in separate bowls or dishes.

**Split** Chinese Grilled Pancakes, spread lightly with hoisin sauce (don't overdo it) and fill with a little duck or chicken, a length of spring onion and a little shredded lettuce. Roll up and eat.

**Makes enough for 4 people.**

**Make a menu match with:** *Fruit Crumble with Ginger, Cardamom and Cashews.*

### FLAVOUR WITH CITRUS RINDS
*You get some wonderful flavours out of the rinds of oranges, lemons and limes. Using these rinds helps you to cut out fat without losing flavour. The trick is not to include the white pith under the skin which is bitter. Use a small zesting tool, a fine grater or peel with a vegetable peeler, removing any white pith with a sharp knife.*

*Carnival Couscous with Chicken*

*Ladies for Lunch*

**Double Baked Soufflés with Smoked Salmon**

**Spring Salad Greens with Favourite Dressing**

**Manhatten Lime Meringue Tart**

## Double Baked Soufflés with Smoked Salmon

*This is my idea of magic – soufflés after all are renowned for their temperamental deflations. Anne Willan demonstrated a great version of this currently fashionable recipe at our cookschool when she last visited. Recipes abound, but here's my version, based around Anne's, rich with the flavours of salmon and herbs.*

TO PREPARE: 15 minutes    TO COOK: 20 minutes, then 5-7 minutes

**60g butter,** plus extra to butter ramekins

**½ cup flour**

**2 cups milk**

**pinch freshly ground nutmeg**

**salt & freshly ground black pepper to taste**

**5 egg yolks**

**100g smoked salmon pieces,** minced

**1 cup tasty cheese,** grated

**¼ cup fresh chervil or other fresh herbs e.g. basil,** chopped, **parsley or tarragon,** finely chopped

**6 egg whites**

**about ½ cup cream**

**a little fresh parmesan,** shaved with a potato peeler

**Preheat** oven to 175°C. Boil a full jug of water.

**Butter** 8 small ramekins and put in the fridge. Then butter again – this prevents mix from sticking.

**Melt** butter in a large pot, add in flour and stir over heat for a minute.

**Whisk** in milk, nutmeg, salt and pepper, stirring constantly until sauce simmers and thickens.

**Remove** from heat and beat in egg yolks, one at a time.

**Beat** in salmon, cheese and half the herbs, reserving rest of herbs for garnish.

**Whip** egg whites until stiff, in a clean dry bowl.

**Add** one quarter of egg whites to sauce and fold in until thoroughly mixed. Add remainder of egg whites and fold together as lightly as possible (If sauce is cold, reheat gently before adding egg whites).

**Fill** ramekins with mixture to top. Smooth tops and run your thumb around edge of dish so soufflés rise evenly.

**Set** ramekins in a deep roasting dish lined with a clean tea towel, so the dishes don't crack.

**Pour** boiling water around them to come half way up the sides of the dishes. Place immediately into hot oven.

**Bake** until soufflés are puffed, browned and just set in the centre, 15-20 minutes.

**Remove** from water bath and leave to cool – the soufflés will shrink back into the ramekins, pulling away slightly from sides.

**Unmould** cooked soufflés into an ovenproof dish. Soufflés can be prepared up to 24 hours ahead to this point and kept covered in the refrigerator.

**Pour** over enough cream into dish to cover base by 1cm.

**Heat** oven to 220°C. Bake soufflés until browned and slightly puffed 5-7 minutes. Sprinkle with chervil, top with a few shavings of fresh parmesan and serve immediately.

**Serves 6-8.**

**Variations:**

Goat's Cheese and Olive Soufflés – in place of cheddar, salmon and herbs, 150g crumbled goat's cheese and half cup of freshly chopped olives.

Blue Cheese and Spinach Soufflés – in place of cheddar, salmon and herbs, 1 cup cooked spinach (all moisture squeezed out) and 150g crumbled blue cheese.

Sage and Lemon Soufflés – in place of salmon and herbs, 1 tbsp minced fresh sage, finely grated rind and juice of 1 lemon.

**Make a menu match with:** *Spring salad greens with Favourite Dressing.*

## Herb Crusted Lamb Racks

*Don't you hate it when you put a fancy crust on the meat and it peels off when you come to carve! Brushing the meat with egg white before you start makes the crust stick. Vary the formula for the crust to suit your own tastes.*

**TO PREPARE:** 10 minutes    **TO COOK:** 15-20 minutes

**2 tbsp fresh herbs,** e.g. rosemary, chervil, parsley, oregano, finely chopped

**1 tsp oil**

**1 medium slice white bread**

**salt & freshly ground black pepper to taste**

**2 lamb racks,** fat trimmed off and bones cleaned

**1 egg white,** loosely beaten

**Blend** herbs, oil and bread to a fine crumb.
**Season** with salt and pepper.
**Brush** flesh side of lamb rack with egg white.
**Sprinkle** over crumb and press on.
**Bake** 220°C for 12-15 minutes until medium rare, and finish under the grill to brown crust if needed.
**Stand** 5 minutes before carving.

**Serves 4-5.**

**Make a menu match with:** *Roasted Garlic Mashed Potatoes and Sautéed Spinach.*


## Sautéed Spinach

**Wash** 2 big bunches of spinach, remove stems and leave wet. **Heat** 2 tbsp olive oil in the large pan, add spinach, grate over a little nutmeg and season with salt and freshly ground black pepper to taste. **Stir-fry** over high heat just until wilted. **Serves 4-5.**


## Brazilian Seafood Stew

*The combination of peanuts or cashew nuts and coconut cream is very Latin. This is a really easy recipe simply requiring fresh seafood to be added to what is essentially a store cupboard sauce.*

**TO PREPARE:** 10 minutes    **TO COOK:** 10 minutes

**1 tbsp oil**

**1 tbsp ginger root,** minced

**2 spring onions,** diced

**2 tsp chilli powder**

**2 tbsp lemon juice**

**1 tbsp soya sauce**

**2 tbsp peanut butter, or cashew butter\***

**1 cup fish stock** (see page 106)

**1 x 400ml can coconut cream**

**600-800g mixed seafood, e.g. prawns, mussels, squid, crab, boneless fish,** diced

**salt & freshly ground black pepper to taste**

**¼ cup fresh coriander or parsley,** chopped

**Heat** oil in a heavy based large saucepan.
**Add** ginger root, diced spring onion and chilli powder and fry for a minute.
**Mix** in lemon juice, soya sauce, peanut or cashew butter, and stir until nut butter has dissolved. Mix in fish stock and coconut cream and bring to a simmer. (Sauce can be prepared ahead to this point.)
**Add** roughly chopped seafood. Adjust seasonings to taste.
**Simmer** 4-5 minutes until seafood is cooked. Mix in chopped coriander or parsley.

**Serves 4.**

**Make a menu match with:** *Perfect Rice or noodles and lightly cooked asparagus.*

*\* To make Cashew Butter, grind or blend roasted salted cashews until pasty, adding a little oil if needed.*

*oodles.* *The pasta of Asia has finally come of age; even the supermarket sells bean thread noodles, Chinese egg noodles, rice sticks and vermicelli. At home in soups, stir-fries and salads, noodles offer enormous scope to the cook. And when it really comes down to it there isn't too much difference between chicken noodle soup à la France and chicken noodle soup made in Asian style – both are egg noodles floating in a broth; it's just the seasonings that head off in different directions. Cook until al dente, like pasta, and use different kinds interchangeably – the exception being bean thread noodles which just need soaking. There are literally oodles of different noodles; here's a primer on some favourites.*

## Glass Noodles

*Otherwise known as bean thread noodles, cellophane noodles or vermicelli. Made from mung bean starch they are incredibly tough in their dried form. I find it easiest to undo the packet and tip contents into a large clean plastic bag, loosening so that a bundle can be easily pulled out, or cut off with heavy scissors.*

**To use,** soak in hottish water for about 15 minutes until they become soft, gelatinous and clear and can be easily broken or cut into shorter lengths. They can then be added to soups, stuffings and gravied stir-fries and absorb lots of flavour from the broth or dressing used. Also great deep fried, puffing up to a white crispy mass, good for the base of salads or stir-fries.

## Chinese Egg Noodles

*Sold fresh and dried, often in portion "nests".*

**Boil** noodles like pasta allowing 2-3 minutes for thin ones and 3-4 minutes for thicker. **Substitute:** any ribbon pasta or spaghetti.

## Instant Noodles

*Sometimes known as ramen, they are available in hanks as well as individual packages.*

**Cook** in liquid, soup or gravy for 2-3 minutes. Useful for quick meal-in-one soups with flavourings like miso.

## Rice Stick Noodles

*Made from rice flour, these flat thin noodles need to be soaked before they are quickly cooked. They tend to exude more starch than other types of noodles when cooked and need to be cooked in plenty of water like pasta.*

**Soak** in hot water 5-8 minutes then drain. If not using at once, mix with a little oil to prevent sticking. **To cook,** drop into boiling water and leave for just 1-2 minutes, until they taste al dente, moving around with chopsticks to prevent noodles from clumping. They overcook easily, so remove immediately and drain and run under water to remove excess starch. Use in soups and stir-fries. Can also be deep fried straight from the pack. **Substitute:** linguini.

## Soba

*Japanese noodles made with buckwheat, these thin brownish grey noodles are traditionally used in soups, and in salads with dressings. Cook like pasta; they take about 7 minutes.*

## Udon

*Very thick hearty noodles with great texture, available fresh from Asian food markets in the chiller. Good for stir-fries and salads.*

**For fresh,** bring to room temperature then pull apart with your hands. Drop into boiling water for 1 minute or stir-fry. **Substitute:** any ribbon pasta.

# Crispy Pizza Crust

*If you like a crisp crust pizza this is the dough for you. It's wonderful to handle, rolls thinly, is very smooth and pliable and has a great nutty taste. In addition to flat crisp pizzas, use it for folded pizzas (calzone), stuffed pizzas or pizza bread. A single recipe makes enough for 10 small pizzas.*

**TO PREPARE:** 10 minutes  **TO COOK:** 15-20 minutes

2 tsp honey

1½ cups water

2 tsp dry yeast

3 cups high grade flour

1½ cups semolina

1 tsp salt

**olive oil and cornmeal,** as needed

**Mix** honey, water, yeast and ½ cup of high grade flour in a big bowl to make a smooth batter.

**Cover**, place in a warm spot, and let rise about 20 minutes, or until a frothy sponge develops.

**Add** rest of flour, semolina and salt to the batter. Knead with a dough hook or by hand until a smooth elastic dough develops (about 5 minutes).

**Add** additional flour, if necessary. The dough should pull cleanly away from the bowl or bench.

**Divide** dough into 10 equal pieces, shape into balls, lightly oil the tops, place on a greased baking tray and cover with plastic wrap.

**Leave** to rise in a warm place until doubled. Flatten the dough very thinly into 18cm circles onto greased baking paper or greased baking tray.

**Refrigerate** until needed. Uncooked bases freeze well.

**To cook:** Preheat oven to 220°C. Transfer pizzas 1 or 2 at a time on their baking paper carefully onto a baking tray. Cover the pizza bases with desired toppings (not too thick). Bake for 12-15 minutes. The pizza is done when the crust is golden brown and crisp. N.B. Pizza Bread topped with only olive oil and herbs will cook more quickly.

**Toppings for Pizzas and Pizza Breads:**

Pan-fried spinach or rocket, roasted garlic, mozzarella and parmesan.

Roasted tomatoes, roasted peppers, fresh mozzarella and olives.

Bacon, sliced mushrooms and olives.

Tandoori sauce, thinly sliced chicken, mozzarella and fresh coriander.

Olive paste, goat's cheese, roasted eggplant, red peppers and fresh mozzarella.

Sliced onions, mozzarella cheese, capers and roasted tomatoes.

Olive oil, garlic, salt, fresh rosemary.

Pesto, sliced eggplant, mushrooms and feta cheese.

Harissa or chilli paste and grated gruyère.

## Chinese Grilled Pancakes

**Place** 2 cups flour in a mixing bowl with $1/2$ tsp sugar and 1 tsp salt. **Mix** in $1/2$ cup water and 1 tsp oil, kneading to form a firm dough. Divide in half and form each half into a sausage. Cut each sausage into 12 equal portions, then form each portion into a ball and pat into circles. **Brush** top of one round with sesame oil then top it with another like a sandwich. Repeat with the other balls to form 12 "sandwiches". Roll out each double stack very thinly to form 10cm rounds. **Cook** on preheated barbecue plate for about 2-3 minutes on each side. **Split** pancakes in half to serve and spread with a small amount of black bean sauce, mayonnaise or peanut sauce, then toppings of your choice. Recipe easily doubles. **Makes 12 pancakes.**

**Suggested filling combinations:**

Black bean sauce, spring onions, cooked chicken or duck.

Peanut sauce, spring onions, mashed hard boiled eggs and alfalfa sprouts.

Cooked chicken, taco sauce and sour cream.

Roasted vegetables and sesame flavoured mayonnaise.

*Beijing Duck Salad Pancakes, page 88*

*Fruit Crumble with Ginger,*

*Cardamom and Cashews, page 103*

# A little sweetness

**The end of a meal,
the chance to indulge
our craving for sweetness.**

Sometimes a slice or platter of freshest ripest fruit will suffice – raspberries topped with a cloud of whipped cream and a dusting of icing sugar, or fresh peaches tossed with toasted coconut, honey and lemon juice. Take fresh fruit uptown with fruit purées folded through stiffly whipped cream in equal parts – the classic fruit fool. Fruit crumbles take our fancy when old-fashioned desserts are on the agenda. We indulge ourselves in upside down apple pie, decadent rice puddings folded through with melted white chocolate and rum soaked raisins and fail-proof soufflés of puréed fruits and white meringue. For holidays and picnics we treat our sweet tooth to portable moist syrup cakes and crunchy biscotti. Whatever the weather or the occasion, dessert looks set to steal the show.

## Harvest Fruit Brûlée

*Fresh fruits topped with a thin layer of rich custard and flash-grilled make a sensational dessert. The custard can be prepared ahead of time and refrigerated.*

**TO PREPARE:** 5 minutes **TO COOK:** 12 -15 minutes

**1 cup cream**

**1 vanilla pod,** split open, or 1 tsp vanilla essence

**pinch salt**

**2 tbsp sugar**

**3 egg yolks**

**1 tsp cornflour**

**5-6 cups sliced mixed fresh seasonal fruits**

**¼ cup muscovado or brown sugar**

**Heat** cream with vanilla pod, salt and sugar until it comes to the boil, in a small pot that will fit over a larger pot. Discard vanilla pod (dry and store in sugar jar).

**Place** pot over another larger pot of simmering water or double boiler.

**Beat** egg yolks with cornflour and pour into hot cream mixture, stirring continually until mixture is lightly thickened and coats the back of a spoon (about 5 minutes). Pour into a jug until ready to use. (Sauce can be made ahead of time and refrigerated.)

**To serve,** divide sliced fruits between 6 ovenproof serving plates. Pour about 3 tbsp custard over each plate. Sieve over with sugar and grill for 3-4 minutes until sugar melts and custard lightly browns.

**Serves 6.**

## Persimmon Sauce

*Try this easy sauce with fresh apricots, mangoes, or paw paw.*

**Boil** ½ cup sugar, ½ cup orange juice and 3 tbsp minced root ginger, stirring until sugar is dissolved. **Remove** from heat. Leave to infuse for 20 minutes. **Halve** 2 large persimmon and remove stones. **Place** flesh in blender and purée till very smooth. **Add** purée to orange juice mix with 2 tbsp fresh lime juice. **Makes 2 cups.**

## White Chocolate and Rum Rice Pudding with Persimmon Sauce

*Cooked in a pot on top of the stove, this rice pudding is dream time. Chunks of semi-melted white chocolate and rum-laced raisins run through the creamy rice base. Make ahead of time – it's delicious served warm or at room temperature.*

**TO PREPARE:** 10 minutes plus 1 hour fruit soaking **TO COOK:** 20 minutes

**½ cup raisins**

**⅓ cup rum**

**½ cup short grain rice**

**3 tbsp sugar**

**1 cup cream**

**2½ cups milk**

**1 tsp vanilla essence**

**½ tsp ground cinnamon**

**¾ cup chopped white chocolate**

**1 recipe persimmon sauce** (see below left)

**Garnish: extra white chocolate,** grated

**Place** raisins in a cup and cover with rum.

**Soak** 1 hour, or microwave 1 minute then stand 20 minutes. Put aside.

**Place** rice in a heavy based pot over very low heat with the sugar, cream, milk, vanilla and cinnamon and cook until the rice is creamy and tender, about 20 minutes, stirring often. Add more milk if mixture becomes dry.

**Allow** to cool a little then stir in the soaked fruits, soaking rum and chocolate.

**Spoon** a little persimmon sauce onto each plate, top with a dollop of rice.

**Grate** over some extra white chocolate for garnish.

**Serves 6.**

*White Chocolate and Rum Rice Pudding with Persimmon Sauce*

Manhattan Lime
Meringue Tart

## Sweet Buttery Tart Dough

*This is a really good sweet tart pastry which has a very crispy crust that does not sog. It is important to use high grade flour otherwise pastry will be too fragile.*

**TO PREPARE:** 10 minutes plus chilling   **TO COOK:** 20-25 minutes

**180g unsalted butter,** room temperature, not melted

**⅓ cup icing sugar**

**1 large egg yolk**

**1½ cups high grade flour**

**finely grated rind of ½ lemon,** no pith

**Cut** butter into 10 pieces – it should be easy to work.

**Beat** or blend together with icing sugar and egg yolk until creamy. Scrape down sides of the bowl and add half of the flour. Beat until crumbly.

**Stop** the machine, scrape down sides of bowl again, add the remaining flour, lemon rind and beat until the dough forms a sticky mass. Shape dough into a flat disc (it will be quite soft) and wrap in plastic or baking paper.

**Refrigerate** for about 30 minutes, until firm.

**Preheat** oven to 190°C.

**Roll** out dough to fit a 28cm shallow pie dish to cover base and sides, or 6-8 individual tart pans. Chill until ready to cook.

**Place** a sheet of baking paper on top of pastry and sprinkle over about 2 cups dry beans or baking beans to weight (this helps the pastry keep its shape). Bake for 10 minutes.

**Lower** heat to 160°C. Remove paper and beans or rice and continue cooking for about 15-20 minutes until base is dry, crisp and lightly golden.

**To Par-cook** pastry for use with fillings that need cooking for 15 or more minutes – proceed as above, cooking pastry for 10 minutes with weighted paper on top, and then 10 minutes uncovered.

**Makes enough for 1 x 28cm tart case or 6-8 individual tarts.**

## Manhattan Lime Meringue Tart

*Inspiration for this yummy tart comes from the excellent little 'Book of Tarts' by Maury Rubin. Use limes or lemons.*

**TO PREPARE:** 10 minutes   **TO COOK:** 5-8 minutes

**1 x 28cm cooked pastry shell** or 8-10 individual cooked pastry cases

**1 recipe Lime or Lemon Curd** (see below)

**6 large egg whites,** at room temperature

**1 tsp cream of tartar**

**1 cup sugar**

**Fill** curd into cooked tart shell to just below pastry rim.

**Place** egg whites in a large mixing bowl. Beat until thick and fluffy. Add cream of tartar, increase speed to medium, and beat until soft peaks have formed.

**Add** sugar, slowly in a steady stream, and continue beating until stiff, glossy peaks have formed.

**Spoon** meringue over the top of the tart.

**Bake** for 5-8 minutes at 200°C until meringue is very lightly browned.

**Remove** from oven and chill for at least 20 minutes in the freezer or up to 12 hours in the fridge.

**Serves 8-10.**

## Lime Curd

**Place** 1 cup sugar and the finely grated rind of 3 limes in a pot with ½ cup lime juice and 200g unsalted butter, cut into 10 pieces. Bring to a boil. **Heat** a larger pot of hot water. **Remove** sugar and butter mixture from heat and whisk in 4 lightly beaten eggs. **Place** pot over larger pot of boiling water and stir constantly until sauce is thickened. Cool and place in a clean container. (It will keep 10 days in the fridge.) Lemons can be used in place of limes. **Makes 2 cups.**

## 90s Tarte Tatin

*This is just so easy and so scrumptious – an ooey gooey pudding which deserves lashings of whipped cream. Everything can be prepared well in advance ready for a final bake off of the pastry.*

**TO PREPARE:** 8 minutes  **TO COOK:** 60 minutes

**1 kg cooking apples,** peeled, cored and sliced in sixths or 2 x 550g cans apple slices

**juice of** $^1/_2$ **lemon**

$^1/_4$ **cup sugar**

**2 tbsp golden syrup**

**1 tbsp butter**

**2 tbsp marmalade**

**250g puff pastry**

**Prepare** apples first. As you slice them, place into a bowl of water with the juice of $^1/_2$ a lemon to prevent them going brown.

**Heat** sugar, golden syrup, butter and marmalade in a medium-large heavy ovenproof pan or paella dish, stirring until sugar has fully dissolved.

**Drain** apples thoroughly, dry well and arrange in a single, slightly overlapping pattern around pan.

**Cook** until apples are semi-tender and coated with caramel. There should be no excess watery liquid in the pan. This will take about 25 minutes. Remove from heat. Dish can be prepared a day ahead to this point and chilled. (If using canned apples they will caramelise in 10-15 minutes.)

**Preheat** oven to 200°C.

**Roll** out pastry to fit top of pan. Place over top of apples, leaving edges unsealed. Cut 2-3 slits in the top of pastry.

**Bake** for about 15-20 minutes, or until crust is golden.

**To serve,** invert tart onto a large flat serving plate.

**Serves 6-8.**

## Greek Lemon Syrup Cake

*The syrup cakes of Greece and Turkey are usually made with semolina which gives them a moist dense texture. This is lovely and light, almost like a sponge.*

**TO PREPARE:** 10 minutes  **TO COOK:** 40-45 minutes

**finely grated rind of 3 lemons,** no pith

**1 tsp cardamom seeds,** lightly crushed

**1**$^1/_4$ **cups sugar**

**6 large eggs,** separated

**1 cup fine semolina**

$^1/_2$ **cup flour**

**1 tsp baking powder**

**juice of 1 lemon**

**recipe lemon syrup** (see below)

**Preheat** oven to 180°C.

**Beat** rinds, cardamom, sugar and yolks until thick and pale.

**Add** semolina, flour, baking powder and juice. Stir to combine.

**Beat** egg whites to stiff peaks and gently fold into cake.

**Pour** into a greased 22-25cm springform tin. Bake 40-45 minutes until a skewer inserted into centre of cake comes out clean.

**Turn** out cake and while hot, brush with lemon syrup, using all of it. Arrange slices of lemon from syrup evenly over top of cake.

**Serve** with whipped cream. Keep in the fridge.

**Serves 8-10.**

## Lemon Syrup

**Boil** 1$^1/_4$ cups sugar and 1$^1/_4$ cups water in a pot for 4 minutes. **Add** 1 very thinly sliced lemon, pips removed, and $^1/_4$ cup lemon juice. **Boil** 5 minutes. **Remove** from heat. **Syrup** will keep 10 days in the fridge.

## Prune and Orange Soufflés

*This is an incredibly easy and delicious soufflé formula needing no complex assembly or production – simply a hot fruit purée folded through stiffly beaten meringue and then baked. Elizabeth David refers to the concept in her 50s edition of Mediterranean food, using 225g of cooked dried apricot purée and stiffly beaten whites of 3 or 4 eggs. It can be adapted with any kind of fruit purée and flavouring – apricots and hazelnut liqueur are also wonderful.*

**TO PREPARE:** 20 minutes    **TO COOK:** 5-6 minutes

**1 cup pitted prunes (150g)**

**½ cup white wine**

**½ cup orange juice**

**finely grated rind of 1 orange**

**3 tbsp honey**

**4 egg whites**

**3 tbsp sugar**

**To garnish: 2-3 tbsp slivered almonds**

**Soak** prunes overnight with wine, orange juice, rind and honey. Or microwave for 3 minutes then stand 1 hour.

**Cook** them in their soaking liquid until soft, then purée until smooth, adding extra sugar if desired to taste. (Purée can be stored in the fridge for 1-2 days.) When ready to use heat purée to almost boiling (it microwaves well).

**Whisk** egg whites stiffly with sugar. Fold the hot purée into whites with a metal spoon until mixture is well combined, working quickly. Spoon mixture into small greased soufflé dishes or cups, piling high to overfill. Put in the fridge if not planning to cook immediately – soufflés will hold 1-2 hours.

**Top** each soufflé with a few slivered almonds and bake at 200°C for 5-8 minutes or until they are lightly golden and well risen.

**Serves 6-8.**

## Fruit Crumble with Ginger, Cardamom and Cashews

*There's crumble and then there's CRUMBLE. Cardamom and ginger with the tropical twist of coconut and cashews are a terrific combination in this easy dessert. Try it also with other seasonal fruits as available – tamarillo and apple or rhubarb and strawberry.*

**TO PREPARE:** 10 minutes    **TO COOK:** 45 minutes

**2 cups cooked apples** or 1 x 550g can

**2 cups fresh or frozen berries,** try a combination of cherries and redcurrants

**¼ cup sugar**

**Topping:**

**1 cup flour**

**1 cup brown sugar**

**1½ cups rolled oats,** smallest available

**1½ tsp cardamom seeds,** crushed

**1 tsp ground ginger**

**1 cup coarse thread coconut**

**Optional: 1 cup raw cashew nuts**

**120g butter,** melted

**Preheat** oven to 170°C.

**Mix** fruits with sugar.

**Spread** into a 30cm x 35cm baking dish or roasting dish.

**Place** dry ingredients, spices, coconut and optional nuts in a large bowl and mix to combine.

**Pour** over melted butter and mix through.

**Spread** crumble evenly over top of fruit. Bake for 40-45 minutes until golden. Crumble can be assembled ready to cook and refrigerated for several hours before cooking.

**Serves 8-10.**

## Spice Trail Biscotti

*This excellent recipe makes three loaves of crisp delicious biscotti. Biscotti are twice-baked biscuits made without any fat and keep well in a sealed container. You can add all manner of flavourings and nuts to the basic mixture instead of those used here – chocolate and almonds are nice. Leave out the nuts and cut thick for babies' rusks.*

**TO PREPARE:** 2 minutes      **TO COOK:** 45 minutes

3³/₄ **cups plain flour**

1¹/₂ **cups castor sugar**

**pinch salt**

**1 tsp baking powder**

**1 sprig rosemary leaves,** roughly chopped

**finely grated rind of 1 orange and 1 lemon**

**1 tsp fennel seeds**

**4 eggs,** lightly beaten

¹/₄ **tsp vanilla essence**

**75g pistachio nuts**

**Preheat** oven to 200°C.

**Mix** flour, castor sugar, salt, baking powder, rosemary, citrus zests and fennel seeds in a cake mixer bowl.

**Add** eggs, vanilla essence and nuts.

**Mix** to form a sticky dough that keeps its shape.

**Divide** into three pieces. Lightly flour bench and roll each piece into a log 4cm wide.

**Place** loaves on greased baking sheets and bake for approximately 25-30 minutes or until firm and pale gold.

**Allow** to cool slightly.

**Reduce** oven temperature to 160°C.

**Slice** loaves diagonally into long thin cookies. Arrange in a single layer on baking trays.

**Return** biscotti to oven for 15-20 minutes until crisp. Cool on wire racks. Store in an airtight container.

**Makes about 45.**

## Oranges with Caramel, Grand Marnier and Spice Trail Biscotti

*This is one of my favourite desserts. It is so light and fresh yet looks stylish and tastes fabulous. It is particularly suitable to serve after a hefty main course like cassoulet. Everything can be prepared ahead of time ready for a last minute assembly. Try it also with kiwifruit.*

**TO PREPARE:** 10 minutes      **TO COOK:** 6-7 minutes

**peel of 4 oranges,** cut into very fine strips, no pith

**flesh of 8 oranges,** no pith, cut in segments or thinly sliced, or use slices of **10 peeled kiwifruit**

**1 cup sugar**

¹/₄ **cup water**

¹/₄ **cup Grand Marnier or Cointreau**

**To serve: 16 biscotti, a little Greek Yoghurt**

**Pour** 1 cup boiling water over peel.

**Leave** 1 minute and drain.

**Repeat** twice – this eliminates bitterness.

**Drain** peel and reserve to one side. Remove and discard pith from oranges and cut into segments, cutting between the fibres. Place in serving bowl and sprinkle peel over the top. If using kiwifruit, peel, slice and place in serving bowl.

**Heat** sugar and water, stirring over low heat until dissolved. Increase heat and boil until mix turns golden.

**Remove** from heat. Pour ¹/₄ of mixture onto a greased tray. Pour rest of caramel over oranges or kiwifruit and rind, then pour over Grand Marnier or Cointreau.

**Stand** 1-2 hours before serving.

**To serve,** spoon a little Greek Yoghurt onto flat dessert plates. Top with oranges and juices, and 2 biscotti. Break remaining toffee into pieces and use to garnish plates.

**Serves 6.**

## Greek Yoghurt

**Mix** 1 cup plain yoghurt, ¹/₃ cup sour cream and 1 tbsp runny honey.

*Oranges with Caramel, Grand Marnier and Spice Trail Biscotti*

**Al Dente** – Cook, usually pasta or noodles, until tender but with some resistance.

**Boil hard** – Cook over high temperature in water, stock or some other liquid so the mixture boils quickly with lots of bubbles. Often used to reduce and concentrate flavours.

**Bruschetta** – Lightly grilled slices of rustic Italian country bread, sometimes rubbed with garlic or brushed with olive oil.

**Chicken Stock** – Use 4-5 chicken frames and some chicken feet and place in a large pot with 1 chopped onion, 2 bay leaves, some parsley stalks and 1 peeled carrot. Add water to come just 1 finger joint above the chicken bones. Bring to a boil, reduce heat to a simmer and cook for 1-2 hours, replenishing water level regularly. Strain off solids. Freeze stock in a covered container or reduce for stock concentrate.

**Chicken Supremes** – Chicken breasts with trimmed wing bone attached.

**Chop** – Cut into small even sized pieces.

**Crush (garlic)** – Peel the cloves of garlic, cut them with a wide knife then chop very finely until almost a paste.

**Crimp** – Use your finger and thumb to pinch pastry together to form a fluted edge as well as seal pastry.

**Crispy noodles** – Deep fried noodles.

**Dice** – Cut into 5mm cubes.

**Finely Chop** – Cut into very tiny pieces.

**Finely Grate** – Use fine edge of grater or a zesting tool to get fine gratings. Used mostly for parmesan or citrus peel. In the case of citrus peels take care not to grate past outer skin, as white pith underneath is bitter.

**Fish Stock** – Use very fresh fish frames and heads; snapper and hapuka are good, monkfish are the best. Do not use heads from oily fish such as mackerel and kahawai as they tend to give a dirty flavour to the stock. Remove gills – these can make stock bitter, and wash thoroughly to remove any blood. Place in a pot with 2 chopped spring onions, a 2cm knob of fresh ginger, sliced, 2 tbsp lemon juice, 2 cups white wine and cold water to just cover. Bring to a boil, reduce heat and simmer 20 minutes. Strain and reduce further to intensify flavour if required. Do not boil longer than 20 minutes in first stage or stock may be bitter.

**Flavour Paste** – A paste which can be pesto, olive paste, sundried tomato paste or simply a purée of herbs with a little oil, which can be spread over meat, chicken or fish before cooking to add flavour.

**Florets** – The small tips of broccoli or cauliflower.

**Fold** – Usually used for light mixtures with stiffly beaten egg whites. Very gently combine mixtures with a large scooping motion, using a big flat spoon.

**Grate** – Rub against a sharp or rough edged grater to produce medium fine shreds.

**Grilling Vegetables** – A wide variety of vegetables can be grilled for an easy accompaniment to boiled rice and noodles. Slice vegetables into pieces roughly the same size – don't cut them too small. Mix with a little olive oil, garlic flavoured olive oil, or pesto flavoured oil and cook on a preheated barbecue, turning frequently. If using dense vegetables such as potatoes, pumpkin or kumara, boil for 5 minutes before mixing with oil and barbecuing.

**High Grade Flour** – Protein content in the flour varies considerably. The higher the protein, the stronger the flour, the less liquid it will absorb. High protein flours are better suited to bread making, pastries and fruit cakes. All purpose flour has a higher protein content than plain flour.

**Infuse** – What happens to your teabag when you pour hot water over it. The release of flavours in a hot liquid.

**Lightly fry** – Heat a little oil (1 tbsp) in a heavy frypan. When it is hot, add food and cook over high heat, turning often until either wilted, softened or lightly browned.

**Mash** – Crush into a fine texture, either by passing through a sieve, or crush with a fork or a vegetable masher.

**Mince** – Chop so finely the ingredients look like a paste.

**Palm Sugar** – A solid sweet sugar cake made from palm trees.

**Peel Garlic –** Use the flat edge of a big knife or bottom of a jar to bash the garlic to break the skin. Peel off.

**Prepare Spinach –** Wash leaves thoroughly and tear off ribs in the centre of each leaf.

**Puha –** A wild edible sow thistle, rich in vitamins and minerals which needs long slow cooking to become tender. Watercress is a substitute.

**Purée –** Blend usually by machine until mixture is fine, smooth and lump free.

**Reduce –** Boil hard until mixture reduces, to intensify flavour and lightly thicken texture.

**Remove Pin Bones –** The line of bones which runs up the middle of a salmon and trout fillet is easily removed by plucking out individually with tweezers.

**Rest –** Stand meat or chicken after cooking to allow juices to disperse evenly. The larger the cut the longer it should rest – allow 2-3 minutes for steak and 10-15 minutes for larger roasts.

**Roasting Peppers –** Preheat oven to 220°C. Place washed peppers on a baking tray or directly onto cooking rack. Cook for 10-15 minutes until skins have started to blister and brown. Transfer to a clean plastic bag or wrap in a tea towel – steam produced helps skins to lift off. When cool remove skins, seeds, stem and inner pith. Peppers can then be stored, covered in oil for up to 2 weeks in the fridge, or frozen in a little oil.

During the winter, it is easiest and far cheaper to buy ready roasted peppers. Auckland based Kato foods produce excellent, quality roasted red peppers which are available from supermarkets and delis.

**Season –** Add salt and pepper to taste. Sea salt is usually coarser than fine salt. It weighs less per spoonful. For everyday cooking use Iodised salt to ensure an adequate iodine intake.

**Segmented –** Usually refers to oranges or other citrus. After removing rind flesh is cut between the membranes to create small segments.

**Separating Eggs –** Crack egg open by tapping shell with a knife. Tip yolk from one half of shell to other, taking care not to break, allowing the white to fall into a clean dry bowl. If using for meringue or where whites need to be stiffly beaten, make sure that no egg yolk breaks into whites and that there is no fat on your fingers.

**Shave –** Use a potato peeler to cut fine shavings.

**Shred –** Cut food into long thin slivers.

**Shuck –** Remove top shell of shellfish e.g. oysters.

**Simmer –** Cook at a very gentle boil - liquid should just bubble a little, not fast.

**Soak Dried Beans –** Sort through dried beans to remove any stones and damaged beans. Place in a non-reactive container with water to cover by at least 2 finger joints. Stand in a cool place 8-12 hours. Drain and cook in fresh water. To speed up soaking, place beans in pot with cold water to cover, boil 5 minutes, then allow to cool in water. Stand 2 hours then drain and cook in fresh water.

**Soak Dried Fruits –** Cover dried fruits with water, alcohol or juice and leave for at least 1 hour to plump up. To hurry up the process, microwave for 1-2 minutes then stand 20-30 minutes.

**Springform Cake Pan –** A cake pan with a loose bottom and a side lever to release.

**Stir-fry –** Cook quickly in a wok or pan, with a little oil and sometimes a little water, using a wide spoon or metal spatula to toss food while it cooks.

**To Cook Chinese Greens –** Slice off and discard tough stem ends and cut up – for baby bok choy cut in half or quarters lengthwise. Place in a pot with $1/2$ cup water and 1 tsp oil. Cover and boil for 2-3 minutes until softened and bright green. Serve at once; they do not reheat well.

**Toasting Nuts –** Either place on a baking tray and bake at 200°C for 10-12 minutes, or microwave on 100% power for 2-3 minutes per cup, stirring every minute.

# Credits

*The job of cooking easy delicious tasting food is made so much easier by having great quality food to start with. John Taylor at Le Broc and Jack Lum are two of the best in the fresh fruit and vegetable business; Jacqui Dixon from Sabato with superb oils, vinegars, pasta and rice; Kato Foods make great roasted peppers and flavour pastes; Kapiti Cheese, superb gourmet cheeses; Grey Lynn Meats, Top Cuts and the Bassett Road Butcher for properly aged and cared for meats; The Remuera Fish Shop and Seamart for freshest seafoods; and Pandoro for lovely breads. These people give us the opportunity to work with and taste wonderful produce.*

*Your food looks better when presented on a range of exciting tableware. There's no need to use a complete dinner set. Buy unusual, individual pieces to add drama to your table. We are very grateful to a number of our friends and local specialist tableware shops for providing us with wonderful serving plates and dishes.*

*AAJA – Herne Bay and Newmarket, Auckland*

*Studio of Tableware – Mount Eden Road, Auckland*

*Milly's – Ponsonby, Auckland*

*Design Design – Newmarket and Ponsonby, Auckland*

*Theme Basics – Newmarket, Auckland*